MARIA and ANASTASIA:

The Youngest Romanov Grand Duchesses

In Their Own Words

LETTERS, DIARIES, POSTCARDS

Chapter One: 1914   P. 7

Chapter Two: 1915   P. 25

Chapter Three: 1916   P. 54

Chapter Four: 1917   P. 143

Chapter Five: 1918   P. 160

Acknowledgments

Many thanks to Eva and Daniel McDonald for contributing some of the 1918 translations; to Anne Lloyd for some of the images and identifications, and Ilya Grigoriev for his assistance at the Russian Archives.

They were the two youngest daughters of the world's most powerful man - Nicholas II, Tsar of Russia. Known to their family and friends as "The Little Pair", a smaller counterpart to their elder sisters, Grand Duchesses Olga and Tatiana who were "The Big Pair". Maria and Anastasia were the third and fourth grand duchesses born to the Russian imperial couple who were anxiously awaiting a male heir instead.

Maria, nicknamed "Mashka" was born on June 14, 1899; Anastasia followed her almost exactly two years later, on June 5, 1901. Close family friends described Mashka as an "angel" who possessed an unusual physical strength. She had dark blue eyes and brown hair, and was generally considered to be the beauty of the family.

Anastasia or "Nastasia", also known as "Shvybzik" or "Shvybz", which referred to her quick and naughty nature, was said to be made of mercury instead of flesh and blood. She was the family comedian who excelled at mimicking those around her, was rather witty and loved to play practical jokes - to the chagrin of her siblings, governesses, tutors and friends.

Although the two little grand duchesses were born into unimaginable wealth, they led extremely modest lifestyles, even sleeping on camp beds in a room they shared. It is clear from their writing that they were rather normal teenagers, who just happened to be growing up in unusual circumstances. They adored their parents, their "Papa" in particular, and loved each other, as well as their little brother who unfortunately suffered from an incurable illness which could end his life at any given moment – hemophilia.

From the grand duchesses' own writing it is obvious that the "Little Pair" possessed sparkling personalities and a keen sense of humor - these traits and others shine through from every written line. Through the girls' letters and diary we are invited into their private world, to follow their daily routines: visits to the infirmary, leisure time with friends, crushes on young officers; and finally the darker period of Grigori Rasputin's murder, their father's abdication, the revolution, and the family's ultimate exile to Siberia and Urals, where they faced their untimely and tragic deaths.

Note to the Reader

This volume focuses on the lives of the "Little Pair" from the start of World War I in 1914 - until their murder in summer of 1918. As the translator of their words, I tried to avoid making too many interpretations or subjective observations in order to allow you, the reader, reach your own conclusions based on what you read. I believe that this is the best way for you to get to know these charming, funny and wonderful girls. I tried very hard to stay as close as possible to the "essence" of their original writing, including the way they structured their sentences, used abbreviations or capitalized (or not capitalized) certain words. Hence, you may notice some inconsistencies in the text, such as spelling or some other apparent errors. Please be aware that these were kept intact deliberately to stay consistent with the original text. You may also notice that I avoided including too much information about the rest of the family, as it is often done in other books about the Russian imperial family members, because I wanted to stay focused solely on the "Little Pair".

This manuscript consists mostly of letters and postcards the teenage grand duchesses wrote to their father and other family members, as well as to friends and acquiantances. Unfortunately both Maria and Anastasia destroyed their diaries when the revolution broke out, but luckily the former's 1916 diary did survive (currently kept at GARF – The State Archive of Russian Federation in Moscow). It is unclear why Maria did not also destroy this particular diary - perhaps it was not as easily accessible to her at the time she decided to burn the others. No matter what the reason, I am grateful that at least one of her diaries survived and we can now read it. Together with Maria's and Anastasia's letters, I included several letters written to them by their father the Tsar, although not as many of those survived: most likely the girls destroyed them along with the diaries.

For almost a century the two youngest Romanov grand duchesses did not get the chance to tell the story of the last four years of their lives. They finally got the chance in this volume, and I feel very priviledged to be their "voice". I hope that by the time you finish this book you will feel you know Grand Duchess Maria Nikolaevna and Grand Duchess Anastasia Nikolaevna a lot better.

Helen Azar. Philadelphia, February 2015.

Chapter One: 1914

Author's Note

In July of 1914, Austria attacked Serbia after a Serbian terrorist assassinated Archduke Franz-Ferdinand. Tsar Nicholas II considered it his Christian duty to stand up for Russia's Serbian Orthodox brothers, which drew Russia into the war. Later that month, Germany declared war on Russia, and in August, Russia began a hasty offensive in East Prussia, to help its ally France, which unfortunately ended in heavy defeat.

By autumn it became clear that the war will not be as quick and painless as many initially imagined. During this time, Nicholas II started to regularly travel to his military headquarters, "Stavka", while Empress Alexandra and her two elder daughters, Olga and Tatiana trained to be "Sisters of Mercy" – military nurses who took care of the wounded Russian soldiers at their infirmary in Tsarskoe Selo[1]. Maria and Anastasia were too young to be certified as nurses, but they too had their own infirmary located within close distance to the Alexander Palace. The girls visited the patients at their infirmary daily: reading to them, helping them write letters, playing games, and generally trying to boost the morale of the wounded soldiers and officers. This was probably the first time the girls faced the darker side of life, and death, and war time became their

---

[1] Town just outside of St Petersburg, where the imperial family established residence at the Alexander Palace.

new reality.

Letter from Maria to Nicholas II

20th September. My dear darling Papa! I am writing to you from downstairs. Mafia[2] and Dmitri[3], who had dinner with us, are sitting here. We went to vsenoshnaya and I prayed for you a lot. Batushka[4] took advantage of your absence and made a speech after vsenoshnaya[5]. During vsenoshnaya it was extremely lonesome that you were not there. I kiss you affectionately and + 2, sleep well and have nice dreams. Your loving Maria.

Letter from Anastasia to Nicholas II

21 September. My precious Papa! I congratulate you with the victory. We went to Aleksei's train today. Saw a lot of wounded. On the way three [of them] died – two officers. Madame Kublitskaya was there. We saw Poretsky, he looks a lot older. Rather serious wounds, so most likely in a couple of days one more soldier will die, they were moaning. Then we rode to the Grand Palace hospital[6], the large one; Mama and the sisters changed dressings, and Maria and I stopped by to see all the wounded, spoke with each one, one showed us a big piece of shrapnel which they removed from his leg, and [it was] a heavy piece. Everyone said they want to return [to the front] to take

---

[2] Maria Pavlovna the Younger, the Tsar's cousin

[3] Grand Duke Dmitri Pavlovich, the Tsar's cousin. Was later involved in Grigori Rasputin's murder.

[4] Priest, literally "Little Father"

[5] Evening prayer service

[6] A military hospital was set up at the Grand (Catherine) Palace as well as separate infirmaries throughout Tsarskoe Selo.

revenge on the enemy! I just came out of the bath. We saw Semenov-Tan-Shansky's sister, who is also working, she is terribly ugly. Aleksei is cheerful, but his leg hurts a bit. At 6 o'clock we returned to the Small Hospital and sat there until twenty to 8. It was so nice and fun. Your little sharpshooter has such pain in his arm that he constantly paces and cannot stay in bed. Sleep well and see me in your dreams. I kiss you 1000 times. Your loving daughter, 13-year-old God's Servant Nastasia ANRPZSG[7]. May God keep you.

Letter from Maria to Nicholas II

21st September. I congratulate you, my darling Papa, with victory. This morning we 4 went to obednya[8] with Mama. Our Batushka and deacon Shavelsky did the service. [We] had breakfast alone, then went to the train with the wounded. Went to Anya's[9] and had tea with her. From there [we] went to the Grand Palace infirmary, Mama, Olga and Tatiana left to do dressing changes. Anya and I walked around all the rooms, where the soldiers were, and spoke with almost each one. Then Mama, Anya and I went home, as Mama had to receive the Sisters of Mercy[10] who are leaving for the front. After that we went to the small infirmary, where your Sharpshooter is [a patient]. There Mama and the sisters changed dressings again, and Anastasia and I went to [see] the officers. I played some game with Popov. After the dressings, the sisters and Mama also played with the officers, so we only returned at dinner time. Had dinner 4 with Mama. Aleksei is fine

---

[7] Her initials plus possibly initials of her nicknames

[8] Morning prayer service

[9] Anna Vyrubova – a close friend of the imperial family.

[10] Nurses

thank God. I kiss you affectionately, my very own darling. Your awfully loving very own Maria. Next time definitely take me with you; or else I will jump into the train myself, because I am so lonesome without out. Sleep well. + MN

"Anastasia and I went to [see] the officers" Maria (left) and Anastasia with officers.

Letter from Anastasia to Nicholas II

22nd September. My precious Papa! Olga just got a telegram from you. I will now go pray with Aleksei, and then finish this letter. It is cold here and sunny. Today we worked at Olga's warehouse. Aleksei feels better, he is cheerful and laughs a lot, so he feels a lot better. 15 new soldiers arrived at my and Maria's hospital, but we have not been there yet. Today we 4 had dinner alone, and Mama ate a little in bed. Mama had a visit from the Sisters[11] who are leaving to the front. Beautiful Countess Kutuzova, Sashka's[12] 3 sisters and 2 nieces were here. Then [also] the hussar's wife, he was killed, I forgot

---

[11] Sisters of Mercy

[12] Alexander Vorontzov

his name, she is not especially pretty. I went to Aleksei's. Returned from Aleksei's, washed up and am writing. I hope that you are sleeping well. I still need to do my homework, how tiresome. We have not ridden our bicycles for a long time and have not passed under the windows of the guard room[13]. This is probably because it's cold. Madam Dedulina said that she has a distant relative Dedulin in the Kekzgolmsky regiment, and he was captured by the Germans in Denzig, and that there are 5 captured officers there. These days we have obednya every day at 9 in the morning at the small church of the Svodny regiment, and Mama was there with Olga this morning. Shura is hurrying my writing as it is time for bed, but of course I do not want to go to sleep. Count Shulenburg brought a German rifle for Aleksei, and also a helmet in a case, a backsword, epaulets of the 147th regiment, and a sash with silver tassels, apparently formal, a piece of shrapnel, and I think, bullets. The rifle is serious, as is the backsword, they are being cleaned, the case too is dirty apparently. Aleksei was so happy. I think tomorrow he is already going back. I must end. I wish you all the best, kiss your hands and feet 1,000,000 times, and wait!!! Your loving with all her heart servant, 13-year-old Nastasia (Shvybzik) ANRPZSG. May the Lord keep you. + Sleep sweetly and see me in your dreams.

Letter from Maria to Nicholas II

24th September. My dear Papa darling! I just returned from Anya's, where Nikolai Pavlovich[14] was [too]. This afternoon Anastasia and I went to our infirmary. 15 men

---

[13] The "little pair" used to pass under those windows so they could talk to the guards, some of whom they had crushes on.

[14] Nikolai Pavlovich Sablin ("N.P.") – The Tsar's Aide-de-Camp

arrived here on Shulenburg's last train. Unfortunately I have to end, as it is now morning and I have to go to my lesson. I kiss you affectionately, my darling, and love you. Regards to Sasha[15] and Nilov[16]. Yours always daughter Maria. Forgive me for such a boring and short letter.

Letters from Anastasia to Nicholas II

24th September 1914. T.[sarskoe] S.[elo] My pearly Papa! Kako Taco Plinta[17]? I just returned from Anya's and Nikolai Pavlovich was there. Today Maria and I went to [see] our soldiers whose relatives were visiting them, [and] we talked to the new ones. Upstairs they prepared for the officers, but it was so cozy, very bright and warm. This morning there was frost on the grass, and on top of ice something like thin ice. I am getting ready to break it. I just took a bath and now sitting all as clean as I don't know what. Again Maria and I worked at the warehouse, and went to Petrograd with Olga and Tatiana. Today Liza[18] is hurrying me to go to bed, but of course I won't go. Maria stayed at Anya's and I am waiting for her because I am alone and bored. It turned out that Count Grancy arrived here. I have not written in my diary for a while, did not have time. So boring. I greet your Imperial Majesty, Hurra! [her drawing was attached here]. Regards to all. Sleep sweetly. May the Lord God keep you. Your loving daughter, the 13-year-old by the name of Nastasia with a patronymic Nikolaevna, and a surname

---

[15] Count Alexander Vorontzov-Dashkov, Hussar Commander

[16] General-Adjutant Admiral Konstantin Dimitrievich Nilov, the Tsar's Flag Captain

[17] Nonsensical, probably an "inside" joke

[18] Her governess

Romanova. Shvybzik. ANRPESG. Artichokes!! And further Rododendron[19]. Uran 1000000 kisses.

Anastasia with her "Papa"

21-22 October. Tuesday. Wednesday. My Good and Kind Papa! We just returned from our infirmary, [saw] a dying soldier and others too. Of course they are such darlings. Saw the officers, where your sharpshooters are. Ortipo[20] was also there, and everyone was terribly happy. So I got up and got dressed and at a quarter of 10 o'cl. we will go to church for Obednya downstairs. I slept wonderfully, did not wake up even once. Now it

---

[19] Again something that appears to be an inside joke

[20] Tatiana's little French bulldog

is 4 degrees below, frosty and overcast. Just now Ortipo was brought to Tatiana, she kisses you and is so busy, such a darling. The eldest sisters are going to Petrograd, and we are staying home. The ice is very thick, children are already running around on it, and grownups too. My stomach wants to eat, it is already growling, asking for food. I think Aleksei slept well, I was only with him for a minute. Now he is having tea, I can hear him. We went to obednya, had breakfast with Mama and the sisters and Aleksei. [We] were remembering you! Right now Maria, Mama and I will go to Mama's train with the supplies. I have to get dressed, such a pity. I kiss you very very affectionately. Hurra! Hurra! Hurra! All the best. Regards to Nikolai Pavlovich and others. Your loving daughter Nastasia. Shvybzik. ANRPZCG Artichokes etc. May the Lord God keep you, my dear Papa.

Letters from Maria to Nicholas II

22 October. My darling Papa dear! I just got a telegram from the regiment. "On this day of regimental holiday the Kazan Dragoons of His Imperial Majesty, raising prayers for the dear health of their beloved Chief, faithfully offer their congratulations and announce a greeting to the 'chief leader' Lord Emperor and our August Chief". I will go to tea now, and then to obednya. Will pray for you and your regiment especially. We already went to obednya and had breakfast. I received a telegram from the regimental ladies, who asked for the infirmary which they founded to be under my patronage. Olga and Tatiana went to Petrograd. Anya and I, with Mama, will review the train-warehouse here on the

vetka[21]. Regards to Nikolai Pavlovich and Sasha. I kiss you affectionately. Your loving, Kazansha[22]. May God keep you. +

23 October. My precious Papa! I'm so sorry that I did not have time to write today. Yesterday afternoon I was with Anastasia and Nastenka[23] at the nanny school, and the children had tea, and I fed them porridge with the nannies, and was reminded of you when the porridge dribbled down their chins and we cleaned their chins with spoons. Today we went to our infirmary, there were many serious head wounds and one in the stomach. Today they all wrote letters home, and a few Siberians could not, so the other wounded helped them.

Maria sharing a smoke with her "Papa". All four grand duchesses used to smoke cigarettes.

---

[21] Train line, literally translated as "branch".

[22] Female version of "Kazanetz" or from the Kazan Regiment. Later she refers to herself as "Kazanetz".

[23] Anastasia Hendrikova, a lady in waiting.

24 October. Just had breakfast. In the morning at 9 o'clock and 50 minutes went to Obednya. Now I will go to our infirmary with Anastasia, and then to the warehouse. Mama went to Petrograd with the sisters. Tatiana will have a committee there and Mama will go to her warehouse. It is very lonesome without you. Regards to Sasha and Nikolai Pavlovich. I kiss your whole body affectionately. I have not seen Demenkov[24]. May God be with you. Your always loving Kazansha.

"I have not seen Demenkov". Nikolai Dmitrievich Demenkov – Maria's "crush".

25 October. My dear Papa darling! I am terribly sorry that I did not have time to write to you. This morning [I had] the obnoxious lessons, as always. Then [we] had breakfast. In the afternoon we went to 4 infirmaries in Pavlovsk with Mama and Aunt Mavra[25], and saw a Cossack who was wounded by a Saxon swine (i.e. their equerry). I am writing so badly, because [I am using] Mama's quill. Just now I washed up, and Liza is combing

---

[24] Nikolai Demenkov was Maria's favorite officer

[25] Grand Duchess Elizaveta Mavrikievna, wife of Grand Duke Konstantin Konstantinovich

my hair. Also today we went to the consecration of Svodny Regiment's infirmary. It is located in the building where the church used to be. A dining room was set up in that room, and moleben[26] was held right there. Where we used to leave our coats is now a room for dressings. Demenkov, my darling, of course was not there. After vsenoshnaya tonight we went to the infirmary, where Iedigarov was [admitted]. I kiss you affectionately, my precious one. Your devoted and loving Kazanetz. Big regards from me to Sasha and Kolya[27]. Gregori[28] was just here. He will remain in Petrograd until you get back. God be with you. +

Letter from Anastasia to Nicholas II

28 October. Tuesday. My precious and good Papa Darling! We just finished dinner. So I am sending you my nice picture. I am sure that you will be very happy. Today I sat with our soldier and helped him read, and it was so pleasant for me. He learned to read and write with us. Two more died yesterday, we even sat with them earlier. This evening Mama is leaving to Pskov with Olga, Tatiana, Olya and Anya. Today it was five degrees of warmth[29], but there was snow mixed with rain and rather strong wind, but not a gale. Right now Ortipo is running after Tatiana around the room. Mama is expecting Maklakov[30] at 9 o'clock and Malama[31] is coming too, this is very nice. I took this picture

---

[26] A prayer service

[27] Grand Duke Nicholas Mikahilovich (?)

[28] Grigori Yefimovich Rasputin

[29] Meaning +5°C

[30] Vasili Maklakov- Respresentative of the Duma

[31] Dmitri Malama was Tatiana's favorite officer

in the mirror, and it was hard because my hands shook. How is Nikolai Pavlovich? Well, I made a stain [on the letter] because Olga butted in. I had seven lessons today, and tomorrow [will have] four or five. Just came in, ending the little governor[32]. It was very pleasant. Yes sirree! I have not written to Aunt Olga[33] for a long time. Olga is hitting Marie, and Marie is screeching, like a foolish Dragoon, such a big fool. Well Malama just got here, is sitting in a chair with the sisters. Olga asked to send one more big kiss to you. I already washed up and now it's time to go to bed. Tomorrow I will finish writing to you. Mama asked me to tell you that she spoke with Maklakov and that he has set everything up and that all is well. She sends you a very big kiss and is sorry she cannot write because she has no time. Tatiana sends a big kiss.

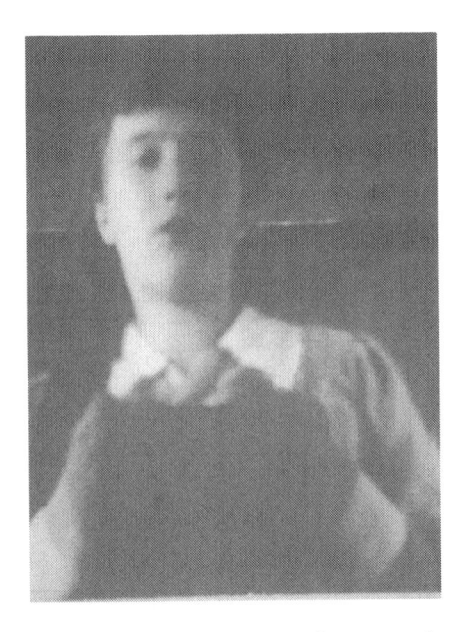

"I took this picture in the mirror, and it was hard because my hands shook."

---

[32] Unclear what this means, possibly related to the dog having an "accident"

[33] Grand Duchess Olga Alexandrovna, the Tsar's sister.

[Continued the next morning]:

Greetings, Your Imperial Majesty. Good morning. I am going to tea. Slept well without Mama and the sisters. I now have a Russian lesson and Pyotr Vasilievich[34] is reading "Notes from the Hunter" by Turgenev to us. Very interesting. Maria and I are working[35], I am using needles, while Maria [is using] a hook. Today it is 5 degrees of warmth, all the snow is gone and it is windy. Right now I will have the arithmetic [lesson]. Maria and I went to [see] our soldiers. One of them does not know grammar, so I will bring him a notebook and a pencil. Then we will probably go to the warehouse. Well it started raining, so nasty. Aleksei got a letter from you and was terribly happy. We already had breakfast. Now Marie and I will go to our infirmary, they brought Nikolaev there, the former officer of the Svodny Regiment. I wish you all the best. Regards to Nikolai Pavlovich. I send you 1000000 big kisses. Your loyal and faithful loving daughter, 13-year-old God's Servant Nastasia (Shvybzik). May God keep you! Come back!!! Soon.

Letters from Maria to Nicholas II

29 October. My precious Papa! This morning, we have lessons, as always. Aleksei has time to write to you today, as he will not have a lesson with Pyotr Vasilyevich. Yesterday evening at half past ten Mama went to the train. Before that Malama was here, he was very sweet. Today all snow melted and the weather is very spring-like, only the grass is not green. Right now it is drizzling a bit. The sisters rode with Anya, Olya and Resin[36]. In

---

[34] Pyotr Vasilievich Petrov - the imperial children's Russian tutor

[35] By "working" the girls generally meant knitting or embroidering

[36] General Resin, Commander of the Mixed Guard

the afternoon, Anastasia and I will probably go to our infirmary. We have this one soldier there who does not say anything, but is awfully sweet. For some reason he loves bracelets and played with one of mine for a long time. We have three soldiers who cannot write at all. One of them learned to read a little with us. We have four officers. One is tall, [he] stinks and is afraid of dressings, and has a wife. Another is fat and not too smart. The third, a regiment commander, always has a bunch of visitors, and the fourth is leaving today it seems. Nikolaev just arrived here from the Svodny Regiment, [he] was wounded, and we are going there now. I kiss you very affectionately and love you. Your Kazanetz. May God keep you. +

30 October. My very own darling Papa! This morning Aleksei's train arrived. Mama was there with Olga, Anastasia and Aleksei. In the afternoon Olga and Tatiana will change dressings again, while Mama will stay home. Mama arrived yesterday at six o'clock. After dinner we 4 went to the infirmary with Anya, where Iedigarov [is]. They were all very sweet. Anastasia and I returned at half past nine. When Olga was speaking to someone for too long, Iedigarov would start coughing loudly, so that she would turn and go to their room. Anastasia and I don't know what we will do this afternoon. I have a cold. Yesterday when we came to our infirmary, suddenly masses of people started coming out of the infirmary (that is the Svodny Regiment officers) and among them was my Demenkov. We got terribly frightened and walked very quietly, so that they would not turn around. Saw Nikolaev, [his hair] got rather gray. He told us a lot of interesting things. In the morning had lessons as usual. Regards to Kolya and Sashka. I firmly shake your hand, in order not to give you my cold. Your Kazanetz. I wrote this letter

before breakfast, but Mama still has not returned from the dressings. May God keep you. +

31 October. My darling Papa! The sisters will take this letter with them. Yesterday afternoon we walked, then went to the Grand Palace infirmary. They already admitted eight officers there. Today we will probably go to our infirmary. I don't know if the new wounded arrived here with yesterday's train or not. The other day I saw my Svodny Regiment sailor from "Ioann Zlatoust" at the gate, and I said hello to him. Ah! I hope that I will see my Demenkov at vsenoshnaya, but I'm afraid that [I will] not, as we are probably going to be standing in the prayer room, and we are too embarrassed to stand in church alone, and walk up to the New Testament. Ortipo is so sweet, and grew bigger in my opinion. Right now I will have an English lesson, how tiresome. I kiss you, your wife, and your two daughters affectionately, and tell the oldest[37] that I will try to call her on the telephone, and if I talk with anyone interesting, I will send her a telegram. Your very own Kazanetz. May God keep you. +

19 November. My darling Papa! Today I am the one writing to you, as Olga and Tatiana just went to Petrograd for the charities. I had lessons in the morning. Mama rode in the train with Olga, Aleksei and Anastasia. Yesterday I was at the Grand Palace with Mama and the sisters, to see the wounded officers and saw that young officer who had a big bed sore on his back. He has a very sweet face. We signed his cards, and now he is waiting for you to return and maybe sign for him too. Right now it is two o'clock. Mama is lying on the couch and writing you a letter, while Anastasia – to Aunt Olga. At 2.30

---

[37] Meaning Olga

Anastasia and I will go to our infirmary. Probably new [patients] also arrived there. At tea I always sit in your chair. Mama got a letter from you before breakfast. Later she will go to the Grand Palace for dressings of two officers. Aleksei is upstairs resting after breakfast. Tomorrow Chakhov is going back to the front. I am so happy that it's a holiday on Friday, so that we will not have lessons, and this is very pleasant. Today during the arithmetic lesson the teacher bent down to see if I wrote something correctly, and broke the chair leg with his weight, and almost fell on me. Well so long, goodbye my Darling. I kiss you affectionately and love you. Your Kazanetz. May God keep you + Regards to Sasha and Kolya and tell the latter to behave.

"The Little Pair" with officers.

22 November. My very own darling Papa! Mama left with the sisters last night at 9 o'clock. Malama had tea with us as he is returning to the regiment. Iedigarov left the

infirmary yesterday [he went] to Petrograd for a couple of days to [see] his wife, and then to the regiment. Mama will arrive tomorrow morning at 9 o'clock, and her train with Loman[38] will already be at the station. So Anastasia, Aleksei and I will go meet her and go directly to the train with the wounded. We are getting 3 new officers at our infirmary. Now I will stop by Isa's[39], who has fever and stomach ache, which was why she did not go with Mama. Well so long, goodbye, my darling. May God keep you. + Your always loving Kazanetz. Regards to your companions.

26 November. My sweet and dear Papa! The other day I wrote you a letter, but tore it up, as the courier already left. I have been going to my infirmary every day. The last train brought some rather seriously wounded [patients]. One of them came to us with a torn lip. Aunt Ella[40] is now here with us, she tells us a lot of interesting things about her journey. May God keep you. Your very own Kazanetz.

30 November. My precious Papa! Mama is now lying on the couch and resting. This morning all of us, 5 with Mama went to obednya and then to change dressings, and Aleksei also watched and counted how many he was present at. After breakfast we took [photographs] with the wounded officers at the Grand Palace. From there we went to the Invalid House, and there Mama gave out St George's medals to several lower ranks. Mama is very tired, and therefore she will not write to you today. We will now

---

[38] Dmitri Loman – a colonel in Nicholas II's own regiment. Was also shot by the Bolsheviks in 1918.

[39] Baroness Sophia Buxhoeveden, lady in waiting.

[40] Grand Duchess Elizabeth Feodorovna, Alexandra's sister. Also the widow of the Tsar's uncle, Grand Duke Sergei Alexandrovich.

have tea with Uncle Pavel[41]. Yesterday at vsenoshnaya I saw my darling Demenkov, while Shvedov was at the meeting. So both Olga and I were very happy. Yesterday afternoon we went to the local infirmary, where Mama also awarded medals. Today after tea Mama will receive the officers, her two Crimeans, one from my regiment and the other from Olga's. I kiss you affectionately, your always loving Kazanetz. May God keep you.+ Regards to Kolya and Sasha.

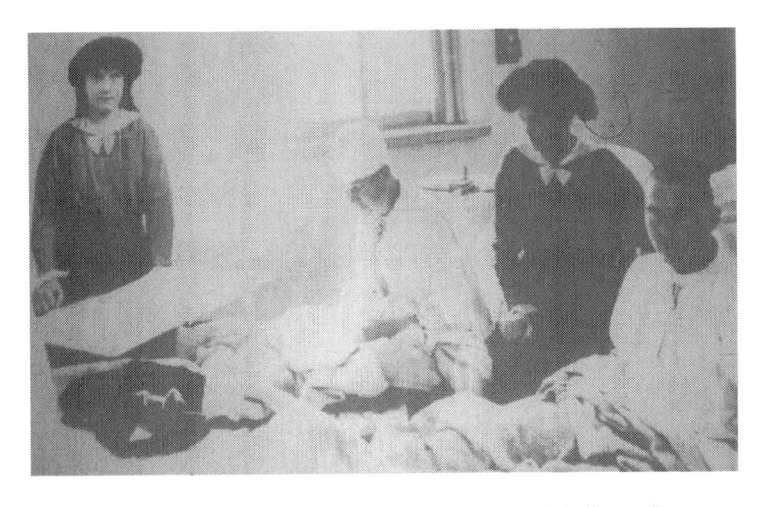

"After breakfast we took [photographs] with the wounded officers…"

---

[41] Grand Duke Pavel Alexandrovich, the Tsar's uncle.

Chapter Two: 1915

Letter from Anastasia to Nicholas II

25 January. My precious Papa darling! Now we are going to church. The weather is wonderful now, the sun shines so nicely. Yesterday Mama's train arrived with the wounded. I wish I were with you! I will finish this letter later as I will be late for church. Well, we just got back from our infirmary. 11 lower ranks arrived there. This one poor young officer, who was injured in the head and therefore cannot speak and can barely hear. I got a letter from a soldier. We went to Glindeman's wedding, he is from the 3rd Sharpshooter regiment. His current wife is sweet and very young. Their wedding took place at the Palace lower church. Of course there was some confusion prior to it, because no one knew where it will take place, and poor Glindeman ran around and did not know what to do. Right now we will have tea, but Mama and Olga and Tatiana have not returned from the Grand Palace yet. They have been there for over an hour already. Regards to Nikolai Pavlovich and to Mordvinov[42] too. Vachnadze can walk already, he is a nizhegorodetz[43]. Well, I think I told you everything we did. Kiss to Aunt Olga. Goodbye, Papa darling. I give you a big kiss, your loving daughter Nastasia Shvybzik. ANRPKZSG. May the Lord be with you! Sleep well and see me in your dreams.

---

[42] Anatoly Mordvinov – Fligel-Adjutant of the Imperial Suite. One of the few who later remained loyal to the Tsar.

[43] From Nizhny Novgorod

Anastasia with Anatoly Mordvinov

30 January, 1915. Tsarskoe Selo. My dear Papa Darling! I thank you very much for the kisses. I write to you so seldom, but [because I do not have] enough time. We just got back from riding. I taught Ortipo to "serve" and today to give paw, she does is so well the darling. Now we will go to our infirmary. In the morning we went to Anya's. The nurses Olga and Tatiana went to Petrograd. Tatiana Andreyevna[44], the one with Aunt [Olga], she wrote to me that when you were at Aunt's you smoked a cigarette, she kept

---

[44] Grand Duchess Olga Alexandrovna's fellow nurse, Tatiana Andreyevna Gromova

26

it and gave the ashes to the officers, and the ashtray was hers. Uncle Petya[45] had breakfast with us. I am happy that I will see you soon. I give you a very big kiss. Your loving daughter, 13 year old Nastasia. Shvybzik. ANRIKZS. May God keep you. Sleep well.

Letters from Maria to Nicholas II

5 April. My precious Papa! I am now sitting near Mama, at her feet lies Shvybzik[46]. Anastasia is drawing. Olga and Tatiana left for the infirmary to [see] Vartanov. When they return, we will go to Obednya. Yesterday after you left, we went home, and then to our infirmary, all 4. The concert was very successful. Delazari[47] was very sweet, and told several funny stories. Then one lady in a sarafan[48] danced a Russian [dance] (she was rather finicky). My Demenkov was very charming, and introduced all the performers to us. The little Shvybzik just made a "governor" on Mama's carpet, and Anastasia is now training him. Today we will see Rodionov and Kozhevnikov. The weather here today is not bad. 15 degrees in the sun. We will take a walk this afternoon there will probably be no one interesting in the guard room. Today none of the sisters will write to you as they will not have enough time. The courier is leaving at 5 o'clock, an awfully inconvenient time. Such a pity that Ilyinsky went with you and not Popov, as you will be in Odessa. So awfully tiresome that you are not here, we could have broken the ice

---

[45] Grand Duke Peter of Oldenburg, Olga Alexandrovna's first husband.

[46] Apparently they also had a dog nicknamed 'Shvybzik", like Anastasia.

[47] Singer

[48] Russian traditional women's dress

together today. Yesterday Anastasia already found two crocuses and a snowdrop[49] under the balcony, not where they were planted, but where they grow on their own. The bell is tolling at "Znamenie"[50] now and it is time for me to put on my hat. I kiss you affectionately, my angel, and love you terribly. Your very own Kazanetz. May God keep you. + Happy 8th April. Regards to Kolya. O., T., A., A.[51] kiss you. I hope that someone good will be at church, most likely Shvedov.

8 April. My sweet good Papa darling! Mama was terribly happy to receive the cross from you, and she is constantly wearing it today. She was lying down on the balcony for the first time today. Anastasia and I rode our bicycles for a bit around the house. The guard on duty today is not very interesting. In the morning it was 20 degrees in the sun. In the afternoon, I walked with Anastasia and Shura[52], and then went to our infirmary. Nikolaev has a toe abscess on his right foot, and they had to remove the nail, so now he has to stay in bed for a few days. [...] I am so happy for you, that you will see Aunt Olga. Do you remember when Tatiana Andreyevena was here and asked for you to come over, back then you didn't think that you would be there so soon. Right now I am sitting near Mama's bed, where she is staying, while Olga and Tatiana are reading. Aleksei wanted to sleep in your spot today and told Mama that he wants to pretend that he is the husband. Yesterday he gorged on black crackers and in the evening he was sent

---

[49] Type of flower which grows in late winter/early spring under snow

[50] Small imperial chapel at Tsarskoe Selo

[51] Stands for the first initials of Olga, Tatiana, Anastasia and Aleksei

[52] Alexandra Tegleva, the head maid at the Alexander Palace.

directly to Derevenko[53]. Olga and Tatiana were in Petrograd today, Olga at the charities, and Tatiana at the committee and [she] took pleasure in dear Neidegart[54]. After dinner I played kolorito[55] with Mama. Now she is reading some English book. Yesterday Kozhevnikov and Rodionov and Kublitsky were at Anya's for tea. Before that they stopped by to bid farewell to Mama, as they were leaving that evening. They were wearing the same shirts as yours. It is so lonesome here without you. I kiss you affectionately, and squeeze you in hugs and love you. Your Kazanetz. Big regards to Kolya. May the Lord keep you. + [...]

"Kozhevnikov and Rodionov and Kublitsky were at Anya's for tea." Vyrubova's little cottage was located just across the street from the Alexander Palace gates. The imperial family often visited there to have tea and play games with officers and other guests.

---

[53] One of the imperial physicians

[54] Apparently she is being sarcastic here

[55] Type of game

Letter from Anastasia to Nicholas II

12 April. My precious Papa! We just finished dinner, and Shvybzik is getting terribly busy with Ortipo. This morning we went to church, as usual. Then had breakfast. Then Olga, Maria and Tatiana rode, the eldest steered themselves. Mama and Anya sat on the balcony. We then went to the local infirmary to [see] the wounded. There are more than a 100 of them there already, and one of Mama's Crimeans was there, black like an agate. Then we also went to the Siberian regiment infirmary, there were 50 lower ranks. This morning it was raining, but later it got wonderfully sunny and kind of humid. At 5 o'clock we went to Anya's, Shvedov, Zborovsky and Demenkov were there, it was very nice. We had tea in the dining room, and almost the entire time there played various games. Shvybzik was there of course. Viktor Erastovich thinks that Shvybzik would make a very good diver. The lake in front of the entrance, there is almost no ice [on it], so pleasant. Olga is playing the piano. So tiresome that [we have] lessons tomorrow. I would like to ride my bicycle tomorrow. I am so embarrassed that my thoughts are so scattered. The "Garden of Eden" was almost entirely under water. It's so nice that you were able to visit everywhere, and the Peremyshel. Mama was terribly happy to get your telegram. Nagorny said that one cannot walk on the ice edges and that the ice is much softer but he could not break it, as he was taking a walk, I think. Mama is reading a letter from the soldiers, one of them is so awfully sweet, here it is: "To Her Imperial Majesty the Empress Alexandra Feodorovna. Dear Madame! Your Easter gifts transformed the soldiers! They were all filled with irrepressible fortitude and courage. Like the Saintly Apostles on the day when the Holy Spirit visited them [and] they spoke in foreign tongues, we too now express our joy though various events, only with subtle

anticipation. Limitlessly loyal to Your Imperial Majesty, the front position warrior of the 183rd Infantry of Pultunsk Regiment, who is always ready to give response." Sweet. Here is one more. I will rewrite it with the [original] mistakes. The letter from 1915, 5 April. "In the first line of my letter, I greet you my dear Mama your Imperial Majesty Empress Alexandra Feodorovna, regards from your little son Fedor Ivanovich I bow low to you and wish you good health from the Lord and from all us Christians wish you long life Received your package on 4 Apr. Received Fedor Ivanovich". There. Probably they will bring Anya here again, as she has been here every day. I will now squeeze [juice] from an orange and then have a lesson. I kiss you affectionately. Your faithful and loyal daughter. Shvybzik ANRPKZS- Nastasia. May God keep you. Regards to Nikolai Pavlovich and others.

"Mama and Anya sat on the balcony." The balcony was a later addition to the west wing of the Alexander Palace, and the family used it a lot, both in winter and summer.

Letters from Maria to Nicholas II

18 April. Papa, my dear darling! Well, how are you doing, can you? I am so happy I saw your glorious Plastuns[56]. We are doing the same as always. Today we went to Vsenoshnaya. Batushka Kibardin did the service while the soldiers sang like angels, so nicely. At the church, there was no one interesting to me, except for our wounded. We just finished dinner. Aleksei came to Mama's to pray. The sisters are dismantling the flowers that were sent by the Yanovs from Livadia. Wisteria and others. While that page was drying, I read Aunt Olga's letter to our Olga. I put Shvybzik on my lap, but he wished to be on the floor. [...]. Mama is sending Anastasia to bed, while she is in despair [because she] cannot find Shvybzik who is missing in action, everyone is shouting and calling him but he does not come, the bastard. Finally we found him after 10 minutes, we were all looking for him under the sofas. Finally Mama decided to bark and Shvybzik barked in response, and it turned out that he was sitting under the couch at Mama's, and he was pulled out with joint effort. I gently kiss the bump on Kotov's forehead and curtsy to darling Litvinov and Chemodurov. Shura is mentally furiously kissing the heel of your left hind leg. I personally embrace and kiss you tenderly. Your faithful and devoted Kazanetz. May God keep you. +. Regards from me to Kolya.

Continuing this letter in the morning at 8 o'clock. I just opened the window curtains and to my joy saw that it is 19 degrees in the sun[57]. Aleksei came to our bedroom, and now he is lying on my bed and playing with Anastasia and Shvybzik. The sisters are still

---

[56] A regiment

[57] They had window thermometers

sleeping, Shvybzik is squealing, probably he wants to see the Governor-General. He has already done that, and Anastasia ran in with the little shovel from the fireplace and picked it up. Well, goodbye, my darling Papa. The sisters and Aleksei kiss you.

13 June. My precious Papa darling! Last night we were at Anya's, [and] Nikolai Dmitrievich[58], Alexander Konstantinovich and Vikt.[or] Erastovich[59] and Skvortsov were all there. It was very nice, we played "Dobchinsky-Bobchinsky" and the Charades. Yesterday afternoon Anastasia and I played tennis. Of course I lost as usual, all three nets. Today we will probably walk to the Grand Palace[60]. The other day we went to the nanny school and squeezed the little children who were already going to bed. We were also at Mama's warehouse, where they rolled bandages, and Anastasia and I had to wear white coats and kerchiefs like everyone else, so that we would both not be too embarrassed. Now we are sitting on the balcony. Anya is now going to [see] Grotov at Krasnoe Selo[61] in the motor. Tatiana went horseback riding, I also wanted to go but have a cold, so did not go. Anastasia, Olga and I were just at the Red Cross infirmary and at the Grand Palace. Today Mama will receive the detachment of British medical motor cars. Well, so long, good-bye, my darling. May the Lord keep you. + I love you very much and kiss you. Your Kazanetz. Regards to Sasha and Kolya.

---

[58] Demenkov

[59] Viktor Erastovich Zborovsky, one of the officers.

[60] Aka Catherine Palace, the official imperial palace at Tsarskoe Selo, located without walking distance from the smaller Alexander Palace

[61] A small military village near Tsarskoe Selo

Maria in 1915

15 June. My biggest darling Papa! Awfully big thanks to you for your sweet and long letter. I thank you once again for the wonderful gifts. Yesterday morning we went to Obednya, then had breakfast on the balcony. In the afternoon, Mama and Anya rode in a carriage, while we 4 in little equipages, which one can drive oneself, I was riding with Tatiana, while Olga with Anastasia. We took the same road that we did with you in the

evening in the motor to Pavlovsk. Georgi[62] crashed his little motor into Mama's equipage, but did not wreck anything. We were riding behind [them] and laughing very hard. Later we had tea with Mama and of course Uncle Pavel, because it was a holiday. The Uncle sang as usual ti-ta-to and then said that he needs to talk to Mama alone, which always happens after he sings at tea. We then got up and went to Anya's and stayed there. Sat on her balcony, and then played in her room. The day was nice in general, but bad because you weren't here. I thank you so much again my darling, love and kiss you affectionately. May Christ be with you. Your Kazanetz. Regards to Sasha and Kolya. I only played tennis once with Anastasia. Anastasia kisses you. She is lying around on the balcony on Mama's couch and drinking coffee.

Letter from Anastasia to Nicholas II

18 June, 1915. Thursday. My precious and sweet Papa Darling! Finally the weather is nice and it is hot, even stuffy. I am hot because I ran around on the gangway. Mama is receiving. Anya just had breakfast with us and left, because she is going to Petrograd to [see] her parents and will return tomorrow. Today it was not pleasant during lessons because it was so hot. We continue to go to the infirmary. Our poor old ensign from the 5th Siberian regiment, arrived three days ago and today he is bad so he probably won't survive, the poor thing. [...] Olga and Tatiana went to Petrograd yesterday. Olga had charities and then they went to Yelagin[63] for tea at Grandmama's. Vasya[64] was there, he is living there [now], and they returned in a motor. Yesterday Nikolai Dimitrievich [sic]

---

[62] Grand Duke Georgi Mikhailovich, one of the Romanov cousins.

[63] Island just off St Petersburg, where the Dowager Empress ("Grandmama") had her main residence.

[64] Prince Vasily Alexandrovich, son of Grand Duchess Ksenia, the Tsar's sister.

Demenkov was on duty. Maria and I rode our bicycles and watched Nagorny fishing and caught only one fish and let it go and it swam away. My fingers are not obeying me and are not writing, the hands are so disgustingly wet. Regards to Nikolai Pavlovich and others. I send 10000000 big kisses. May God keep you. Your very own loving loyal and faithful Nastaska. Kaspiyitz[65] 148 Shvybzik ANRTKZS. Aunt Olga wrote that "Daphne"[66] died, poor thing, and she and Emilia Ivanovna buried him and cried.

Yelagin Palace: "... They went to Yelagin for tea at Grandmama's."

Letter from Maria to Nicholas II

19 June. My precious Papa darling! This afternoon I saw a few children swimming in the river and I, much like you, wanted to go swimming too. Aleksei is line fishing almost

---

[65] Anastasia was the honorary chief of the Kaspiysky Regiment

[66] Olga Alexandrovna's dog

daily now at the pond near the elephant[67]. I forgot to tell you that today we 4 were at Mama's Invalid House and saw the two Cossacks from that Kuban regiment that used to be here. One [of them] was old with a beard, both very sweet. They brought two new officers to our infirmary, from the 5th Siberian Infantry Regiment, one heavily [wounded]. Your letter from Dushkinsk is sitting here at night on the table, and every evening I am happy to [see] it. May God keep you. I kiss you affectionately, same as I love you. Your Kazanetz.

Letters from Anastasia to Nicholas II

22 June, 1915. T.[sarskoe] S.[elo]. My sweet and dear Papa Darling! I am touched every time you send kisses to us in Mama's letters and telegrams. It is now sunny and warm here. My and Maria's cots are sitting in the middle of the room and it is much nicer to sleep here and now our windows are open so it is very pleasant and cozy, but it is much nicer on the train. Yesterday we went to the Grand Palace infirmary and saw your Plastun and he told us that you talked to him and he was very confused, I think they will operate on him, although this is not definite. In the evening Mama rode in the motor with the sisters, while I went to bed. Yesterday we went to Anya's. Viktor Erastovich, Nikolai Dmitrievich, Zolotarev, Fedyushkin and Rogozhin were there. He is very sweet but of course the first time he was very embarrassed, but it was fine. During tea at Anya's yesterday we all sat on the balcony and it was very warm. The curtains were drawn because people were looking inside, but this one lady with a child in her arms was passing by and at this time we all went silent for some reason, and the boy said "Mama

---

[67] Aleksei had a pet elephant kept in the Alexander Park

I want ah ah" and repeated it. We thought that no one heard but everyone heard and we were dying of laughter, [we] hooted for a long time, then went silent and then were dying again until everyone had tears [in eyes], while Demenkov did not hear anything and thought we were laughing at him, and then Viktor Erastovich explained to him [whispering] in his ear. Yesterday before that, Kostya and Tatiana[68] had tea. They were very merry. Kostya is leaving soon and this is why he was here, and Tatiana [was here] just for company, but she had the medal with her. I am now going to [have] a lesson then will finish writing. Well, we already had breakfast, but Mama did not return from the infirmary for a long time, only came back at half past one. Mama is now receiving. These evenings they sit on the balcony until 11 o'cl. with the lamps [lit], and the sisters say that it is very cozy, but I have not yet seen it. We will go to the warehouse in the afternoon, to roll bandages – this is fun and various lady acquaintances are there. I hope that you will return soon. Sometimes we study on the balcony, and once [we] went out to the garden, while they were laying wires for the lamp. Regards to your companions. May God keep you. Sleep well. Your loving from her heart. Your loyal and faithful. Nastaska. Kaspiyitz. ANPRTKZSG.

---

[68] Children of Grand Duke Konstantin Konstantinovich (KR).

"My and Maria's cots are sitting in the middle of the room and it is much nicer to sleep here..." All imperial children usually slept on these types of camp beds, and even took them into exile with them. This photo is from the girls'room in Tobolsk, Siberia, in 1917.

22 August. My dear and sweet Papa Darling. I wish you lots of well-being, and everything good and joyful, and that you are healthy and happy to everyone's joy. We will all pray for you here, for you to be able to bear everything easier. Be well, do not tire yourself out. God will help. Sleep well. May the Lord keep you; Your Loving daughter Nastenka. Shvybzik. Antikz.

Letter from Maria to Nicholas II

26 August. My precious Papa darling! I went to Obednya and molebna with Mama and Anastasia, the Batushka gave a wonderful sermon. It all lasted 1 hour 45 minutes. Olga and Tatiana went to Petrograd and then they will have tea at Grandmama's on Yelagin. I was just at our infirmary with Anastasia. It's so nice that everyone now knows that you replaced Uncle Nikolasha[69], and now you probably feel a lot more peaceful. Well, so long, goodbye, my angel. May Christ be with you. + Your Kazanetz.

Letters from Anastasia to Nicholas II

26 August, 1915. Tsarskoe Selo. My dear and sweet Papa Darling! I am sitting on the couch near Aleksei as he is having dinner with M. Gilliard[70], while Maria is running around like crazy. I can now go to the infirmary but the weather is so nasty and cold that I stay inside[71]. This morning Ostrogorodsky[72] came to see me, but Maria and I were still in bed, then Maria covered herself with the blanket, then he entered and listened to my [lungs], but when he finished I quietly uncovered the blanket and Maria had to climb out, and she was very embarrassed. But as soon as the door was shut, I was dragged down to the floor. We did not do anything interesting in the afternoon. Olga and Tatiana went to the city, while Maria and I went to our infirmary. The officer was awfully funny as usual. Then we sat with Aleksei, when we have time we [always] sit with him [....]

---

[69] As Commander-in-Chief of the Russian army. Grand Duke Nikolai Nikolaevich ("Nikolasha") held that title until that time.

[70] Pierre Gilliard - the French tutor

[71] Anastasia was sick with a cold

[72] One of the imperial physicians

27 August. I am still in bed while Mama and the sisters are going to church, I would like to go too, I already wrote to Mama to ask[73], but I don't know what the answer will be. Luckily today there is no wind and the sun is peeking out a little. Maria and I continue to sleep in the middle of the room and I don't think we will move from here as it is much better. In the morning we went to Obednya and then to Mama's infirmary. In the afternoon we rode with Mama and Anya and ran into horrible old ladies [...] Now we are sitting around and Uncle Pavel will be here for tea. Maria was delighted because as we were leaving church, the fat Demenkov was standing there, but no other good people were there. Aleksei is playing now with the little Aleksei and Sergei. I am sorry but I have to go to tea. All the very best. Regards to Nikolai Pavlovich from me. Sleep well. Do not tire yourself out too much. I wish you all the best. May the Lord be with you. I kiss you 10000000000 times. Your loving loyal and faithful daughter. Kaspiyitz. Nastaska. ANRIKZS.

---

[73] The imperial children often wrote notes to their Mama and she would respond with a note too.

"Maria was delighted because as we were leaving church, the fat Demenkov was standing there..."
Nikolai Demenkov is standing on the left. Olga and Tatiana are greeting members of the suite. Judging by height, it appears that Anastasia is next to Olga (blocked).

4 September, 1915. Tsarskoe Selo. My Sweet and Precious Papa Darling! This afternoon we went to our infirmary. There was a concert. Delazari sang with some three [people], then a young lady danced alone, who danced and sang and also the little man who was at Anya's in the winter, he told awfully funny stories, so everyone was dying of laughter, but he himself did not laugh at all, I cannot remember his name for anything, but if I remember I will write it. Also Nikolai Dmitrievich was there, he was very fat and wearing a blue tunic. The soldiers loved it so they applauded with all their might and our

funny officer made them yell out "bis". I am sitting here with your old cigarette, which you once gave me and it's very tasty[74]. I thank you so much for all the kisses you sent us through telegrams and letters. Today Mitya Dehn is having breakfast here. Yesterday I received one of my officers, and he brought me a report from my regiment. Very interesting. He was not wounded, they just gave him leave for a few weeks and he is already going back. He says that luckily now the wounded officers are starting to return to the regiment, but that there are two wounded in Petrograd. It is so dark now that one has to light a lamp, and this is so tiresome. You probably see Viktor Erastovich from afar? – then I am envious of you. Oh! I remembered, his name is Sladkopevtzev, he is smaller than I am, I noticed with pride. Now I must go do my homework. Big regards to Nikolai Pavlovich. I wish you all the very best. May God keep you. Your loving loyal and faithful Kaspiyitz. Kiss. 1000 times.

Letter from Nicholas II to Maria

Mogilev. 12 September, 1915. My sweet Marie, I thank you so much for your letters, which always make me laugh, from what you write as well as the amount of mistakes in them. I am happy for you, that N.D.[75] is staying in Tsarskoe Selo, but because of that he lost his job at "The Worker". Have you recently been to Peterhof with Mama? I love to reminisce about our trips there on holidays during the summer. Here on the Dnepr, I had from the beginning wanted to row in a boat, but have not been able to do it for some reason, only was able to cross the river twice in a ferry, together with the motors. I

---

[74] Anastasia (and her sisters) smoked. At the time it was believed that cigarettes were healthy.

[75] Demenkov

have very little time and therefore must end this letter. I give you a big hug my dear Kazanetz. May Christ be with you!   Your Papa.

Maria with "Papa"

Letter from Anastasia to Nicholas II

13 September, 1915. Tsarskoe Selo. My sweet and Dear Papa Darling! I am so sorry that I did not write when it was my turn, but I did not have even a minute of time. I was so happy that you wrote, that you saw V.E. and of course I was envious of you. Three days ago Tatiana Andreyevna Gromova was here. She is going to [see] Aunt Olga in Kiev on Tuesday, she is very happy to be going. It is raining now and windy and cold, so the weather is stinky and we have not yet decided what we will do, although probably Maria and I will go to our infirmary. What we did to Monsieur Gilliard yesterday, it was

horrible, we pushed him with [our] fists, he really got it good from us! Olga received a long letter from Mordvinov. He remembered how the sisters climbed out of the motor and how he was so desperate. Such filth, in my and Marie's bedroom a mouse is scurrying around, and I saw it this morning and heard how it was scratching during the night. Today is already three weeks since you left – so long! It is so lonesome without you! The lessons continue, but [we] won't have any on Monday because it is a holiday, so it's very nice! Well, we went to our infirmary, and then we four walked in a light rain, the weather is unpleasant. Three of our wounded from the Svodny Regiment returned there, and I saw them here in the round hall on duty. I am now sitting at Mama's in the big room, and Anya is reading aloud to Mama. We just had tea, and now we are going to church, and unfortunately I have to get dressed. Regards to Nikolai Pavlovich. May God keep you. I give you 100000 big kisses. Your loving loyal and faithful. Kaspiyitz.

Letter from Maria to Nicholas II

15 September. My precious Papa darling! I squeeze you in a hug and kiss you for your dear letter, which I was not expecting to get. We just finished breakfast. I will go walking with Olga and Anastasia. Hope to walk by the guard room, in case N.D.[76] is there. In the morning we had lessons. These last couple of days we went to Obednya at the lower church, as the sisters went to the infirmary right after Obednya. Therefore, of course N.D. was specifically at the upstairs church, and Anya saw him. Rather weak: "Go to sleep, the achievements of fame, everyone, sleep forever"[77]. These days Aleksei is

---

[76] Again Demenkov

[77] She seems to be quoting some poetry

building a fire again. We walk occasionally, but usually in the afternoons we go to the infirmary. Yesterday we went to the Nanny School and squeezed the children. There is this one refugee child, she is only two years old. Her mother died. She is so cute, but speaks Russian badly and calls her nanny Mama. My medical train brought her. These days almost all the medical trains pick up refugees if they have room. Right now we are having tea. Took a very successful walk. N.D. was on duty and we talked with him very nicely through the window. We walked to the Caprice[78] and walked up the stairs. You know [a diagram drawing]. And then, when we got up there, Olga took her parasol and attacked one of the windows viciously, and broke 3 glass panels, then gave me the parasol, and I broke a window too and Anastasia [did] too. It is probably so pleasant for you to have Uncle Misha[79] there with you. Tell him that I kiss him lots. Are you still playing kosti[80]? Tomorrow Aunt Ksenia[81] and Uncle Sandro[82] will have breakfast with us. Olga is reading a newspaper now, while Mama is talking to Anya. Our weather is rotten. Right now it is foggy. Well, goodbye for now, my dear darling. May Christ be with you. + Your Kazanetz. Regards to Kolya and Sasha. I kiss you and Dmitri.

Letters from Maria to Nicholas II

3 October. My precious Papa! Well this time I think you don't feel as empty. I am so happy for you, that you saw the 21st Corp. We are the same here: ride with Mama in the

---

[78] A structure in the Alexander Park, something like a bridge or an overpass.

[79] Grand Duke Michael Alexandrovich, the Tsar's brother.

[80] A game of dice, literally translates as "bones"

[81] Grand Duchess Ksenia Alexandrovna, the Tsar's sister

[82] Grand Duke Alexander Mikhailovich, Ksenia's husband

afternoons, and visit the infirmaries. This one officer transferred to our infirmary from the Red Cross, his name is Shakh-Nazarov. He is very appetizing, dark with a moustache, and in general I approve of him. He was a patient in Pskov before, at Maria's[83] infirmary. We just had tea. In the afternoon we rode around with Mama and Anya. Olga and Tatiana are cleaning the instruments now, before vsenoshnaya. This evening Grigori[84] will be at Anya's. Yesterday morning [we] talked to N.D. through the window. Today I will probably not see him, as we will not be at Vsenoshnaya in the Sobor[85]. I hope that Mama will not bring us to the consecration tomorrow, as there will be so many people and relatives, and so little room, it will be stuffy and one won't be able to pray. Well I must end now, as I will be trying on some dress, [which is] awfully tiresome. Well, goodbye my Papa, darling. I kiss you affectionately, like I love you. Your Kazanetz. May Christ be with you. + Regards to Kolya. We saw Uncle Pavel's wife[86] taking a walk.

7 October. My Papa darling! I am writing out of turn, as Tatiana did not have a chance [to write] because of Petrograd. We, with Anastasia, deigned to visit the warehouse and roll the bandages, then went to our infirmary. A young officer from my regiment was supposed to arrive there, [he was] wounded in the leg in the 25th September attack. He said that lately the regiment has all been on horseback. He is really young, 18 and a half years old. He was presented to me on the 1st of June with two other officers, when he graduated from the Nikolaevsky Cavalier School. We only just consecrated the

---

[83] Again Grand Duchess Maria Pavlovna the Younger, who was also a Sister of Mercy

[84] Again Rasputin. The imperial family mostly saw him "at Anya's"

[85] Feodorovsky Cathedral in Tsarskoe Selo

[86] Countess Paley, the grand duke's mortganatic wife.

cemetery church with Mama, and already two officers died at our infirmary and the Grand Palace infirmary. I must end now as they came in to see if we have a letter for you. I love you very much and kiss you and Baby. + Kazanetz. Regards to Kolya.

31 October, 1915. I am writing to you from the bedroom. Just had tea, the sisters are still sitting at Mama's. This morning [I] had lessons, and in the afternoon rode with Nastenka. Went to our infirmary with Anastasia, and she took [pictures] of our wounded officers. Two of them have St George's crosses. The snow is almost all gone, it is so strange to see grass again, and it seems as though Nature made a mistake and thinks that it is Spring already. In the morning I walked with Shura, [we] walked by the guard room, but did not see anyone, hopefully will see them tonight at vsenoshnaya. Probably Dmitri is doing lots of foolish things and talks [foolishly] too, kiss him for me. The other day an Englishwoman had breakfast with us, she came to Petrograd to establish an English infirmary in Dmitri's house. We are not really doing anything interesting. I will think of you at Vsenoshnaya, how you are now standing at church, and will pray for you. Nothing more to write, therefore I will end. I kiss you affectionately, like I love you. Your Kazanetz. May Christ be with you. + Regards to all of yours and Kolya.

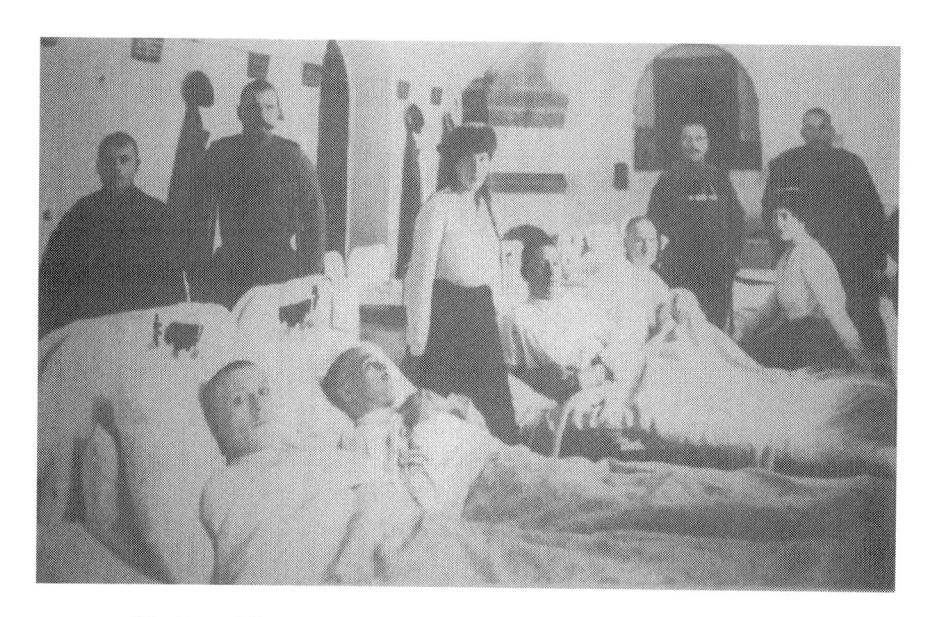

"Went to our infirmary with Anastasia, and took [pictures] of our wounded officers."

Letters from Anastasia to Nicholas II

1 November. My sweet and dear Papa Darling! It is very lonesome here without you. We just went to Vsenoshnaya and already had dinner with Mama. The snow melted already but the Gale is blowing with all its strength, and this is not very pleasant. Well, I am starting a new day. In the morning we went to Obednya as usual. Skorikov, Paleny and Kalashnikov were there. Today is the holy day of Kozma and Damian[87]. We rode in the afternoon, then [we] went to the sisters' Palace infirmary. There was a concert they played the balalaikas, the Tolstoys and many other acquaintances, it turned out very nice. We returned just now. It was raining, but 4 degrees of warmth and very slippery. I can imagine very well how you have dinner and breakfast and imagine all your

---

[87] Saints of physicians and surgeons.

companions. I am writing to you and Aleksei at the same time. I am hurrying because I now have to do my boring homework. "Go to sleep, achievement of fame, all go to sleep!!!" Olga is resting now, while Maria is winding up the gramophone, this is pleasant. All three sisters smooch you a lot, and I do too of course. 100000 big kisses, your loving loyal and faithful Kaspiyitz. Sleep well +.

6 November, 1915. Tsarskoe Selo. [...] Everything is the same here, just lessons and nothing else except the infirmaries where we go almost daily [...]

Letter from Maria to Nicholas II

13 November, 1915. My dear Sweet Papa! Heartfelt wishes for Grandmama's[88] birthday and the wedding anniversary. We had tea at Grandmama's, and I think will go see her again tomorrow. She is very happy with her trip to Kiev and told us that she visited some infirmary every day. Right now [we] will go riding with Nastenka. Then Anastasia and I will go to our infirmary. Yesterday they brought 7 lower ranks there from the train. Rather seriously wounded, we have not seen them yet. Anastasia is sitting next to me, reading something. I have not seen Nik. Dm. It is rather boring for 2 weeks already. Since they had put a couch in the sisters' bedroom, it became much cozier, I kiss you and Aleksei affectionately. Your Kazanetz. Regards to all. Our arithmetic teacher is healthy again and is coming to [teach] us again.

Letter from Anastasia to Nicholas II

---

[88] Dowager Empress

29 November, 1915. Tsarskoe Selo. My dear Papa Darling! We just had breakfast with Lolo Dolgorukaya[89] and I ran from there in order to write to you. Nothing much happened except that we went to Anya's yesterday and Viktor Erastovich and Nikolai Dmitrievich were there. This was after dinner at 9 o'cl. Well that was nice. And this morning we went to Obednya and ran into Viktor Erastovich. He said that Shvedov arrived here. Before Obednya Gulyga came over to bid farewell to Mama, he is leaving today too. Well that is all the news, and the rest is the same as usual. Right now it is snowing hard and is 10 degrees below. Yesterday Maria Pavlovna the Younger had tea with us and looked very adorable because she has curly hair, they curled it for her and it looks very good on her, so we approved. Yesterday during our ride we ran into Countess Paley, alone in Pavlovsk on skis, it was so cute, she could hardly move her legs. When we rode past her, we hooted with laughter a lot and for a long time, but of course she did not see or hear us. Tell Aleksei that "Joy"[90] sends kisses and misses him a lot. He came to us this morning and sat near us and was so sweet but sad. Does the door from your study to the white hall creak? Regrettably I must end. I feel sorry that this letter is so boring, but we never do or see anything interesting, but continue putting on "Vova Has Adapted"[91] and sing the same things we did when you were here. I send you and Aleksei a big kiss and squeeze you in my modest embraces. Your loving loyal and faithful Kaspiyitz.

---

[89] Countess Olga Petrovna Dolgorukaya

[90] Aleksei's pet spaniel

[91] Probably name of a play.

"Your loving loyal and faithful Kaspiyitz."

Letters from Maria to Nicholas II

1 December. My dear precious Papa! Right now I am sitting on the floor in Mama's study, while she is lying on the couch. Anya is sitting in your arm chair, while the sisters are sitting on chairs and working. We just attended the panikhida[92] for Sonia[93]. Her little housemaid Ustinia was crying terribly. Tomorrow Olga and Tatiana will go to Petrograd, the former for charities, and the latter for a committee. I kiss you and Aleksei very affectionately. Your very own Kazanetz.

---

[92] Prayer service for the dead.

[93] Princess Sonia Orbeliani, a friend of the Empress who died after a long debilitating illness.

30 December. May the Lord bless the crest of this new year! I hope this year will bring you, my dear Papa, many happy days. It is so tiresome that we will not see you on the first day of the New Year. In general it is always very boring for us without you. Well, I will finish writing now, or else your imperial eyes will start hurting from reading on this red paper. May Christ be with you. + My dear, I squeeze you tightly in my hug. Your Kazanetz.

Maria (left) and Anastasia posing with their wounded.

Chapter Three: 1916

Maria's diary entries

1 January. In the morning went to Obednya. Had breakfast 5[94], and Mama stayed in bed. In the afternoon went to our infirmary with A.[nastasia]. Had tea 4 with Anya near Mama's bed. Read. Had dinner 4. After dinner Mama came out to the work room and lay down on the couch. Anya was here. Lilies of the valley from Kiki[95].

2 January. In the morning went to Obednya with A[nastasia]. Had breakfast 5. Mama stayed in bed. In the afternoon 4 went to the G[rand] P[alace] and rode in a motor. Had tea 4 with Anya near Mama. Went 4 to Vsenoshnaya and the same had dinner. In the evening Mama was lying on the couch. Anya was here.

3 January. In the morning 4 went to Obednya. Had breakfast 5. Mama was lying down in bed all day. In the afternoon 4 with Nastenka rode in a troika[96]. Went to Kokorevsky infirmary. Then went to our infirmary. Had tea 4 with Anya near Mama. Read. Had dinner 4. Mama was lying down on the couch. Kiki and Anya were here. Before that played with O[lga], A[nastasia] and A[leksei] in Mama's large sitting room with toy revolvers in the dark.

---

[94] When Maria refers to "5" she generally means all four siblings including Aleksei, when she says "4" it just means the four sisters.

[95] Nikolai Pavlovich Sablin's nickname

[96] A fancy sleigh drawn by three horses

Anastasia Hendrikova ("Nastenka") in court dress. "In the afternoon 4 with Nastenka rode in a troika"

Letter from Nicholas II to Maria

I.[imperial] Headquarters. 3 January, 1916. Sweet Marie, I thank you for the little note on red paper, which Teternikov brought to me just before the New Year. I am very touched by your consideration. Regrettably I don't have gymnastics here and have no one to squeeze, not even you. Today I found a shovel in the garden and worked in the snow really well. While I walk I look at those driving and walking by, and sometimes see very funny things! I squeeze you in a tight hug. Your Papa.

Maria's diary entry

4 January. In the morning [we] went to the Palace hospital. Had breakfast 5. Mama is in bed all day. In the afternoon went to the G[rand] P[alace] with O[lga] and T[atiana]. Rode in a motor and got stuck in the snow, so the Cossacks dug us out. Had tea 4 with Anya near Mama.

Letter from Maria to Nicholas II

4 January. My precious Papa! I am writing to you in the morning. Anastasia is sitting on the couch near the fireplace and drawing something. We completely changed our room, the cots are back in their old place, while the screen went elsewhere, I won't be able to describe to you very well where everything is. You will see for yourself when you get back, which I hope will be very soon. This morning at 9 o'clock [we were] at the Grand Palace infirmary, we haven't been there for a terribly long time. And yesterday we went to the Kokorevsky infirmary, your three Yerivantzy[97] are patients there. Day before yesterday we were laughing awfully hard. The old Aunt Olga[98] called our Olga, in order for her to ask this one solider from the Svodny regiment to come over and visit her patient from the same regiment. Well, Olga immediately called the guard room, the guard on duty turned out to be Kulyukin, and he asks: "who is on the telephone?". She answers "Olga Nikolaevna". "Which Olga Nikolaevna?" – "Olga Nikolaevna, don't you know?' The one who lives above you". – "I don't understand anything" – "Grand Duchess Olga Nikolaevna, do you hear me?" – and starts to guffaw madly, so he got hurt and said: "Young lady, this is a service telephone, and practical jokes are not

---

[97] From the city of Yerivan

[98] Grand Duchess Olga Konstantinovna, queen of Greece.

appropriate here", and hung up. Olga left. Then in 5 minutes, Tatiana comes over and makes a call; he recognized her, and she told him everything. Yesterday at obednya Kulyukin comes over and asks Resin to apologize to Olga for him, but that he wasn't expecting that she would call so he thought that someone was playing a practical joke. Because Mama stays in bed, we have breakfast and dinner alone. Well, so long, goodbye. Right now I need to go to breakfast. I squeeze you tightly in a hug and love you. Your Kazanetz. Regards to everyone who is with you.

Maria's diary entry

5 January. In the morning went to church with O[lga], T[atiana] and Al[eksei]. Mama is in bed. In the afternoon walked around the city with T. and Isa. Had tea with O., T. and Anya near Mama. Went to vsenoshnaya with O., T. and Aleksei. Had dinner 3 and Mama [was] on the couch. Anastasia was in bed as she has a cold, she has high fever. Got a letter from Darling Papa.

Letter from Maria to Nicholas II

6 January. My very own dear Papa! I am awfully grateful to you for your dear little letter. I was not expecting it. Right now Anastasia is lying down and having breakfast, Olga and Tatiana were with me at the lower church for Obednya at 9 o'clock, then the sisters and Aleksei went to the infirmary, and I went to take a walk. Today it is 4 degrees, so it is nice to walk. Such a pity that I could not visit you, we could have shoveled snow together. – Such a pity that I am not a boy. Bad things keep happening to us when we ride in the motor. There is so much snow that we drive off to the side of the road and get

stuck in the snow and the hetmans dig us out with shovels. This already happened three times, [it is] rather tiresome and it feels like the motor is turning over to its side. Today we will probably drive to the Grand Palace. Anastasia is already awfully tired of staying in bed, it is particularly tiresome on a holiday. The other day we saw little Olga from the Crimea at Trina's[99]. She was the one who ducked down a lot when we played tennis, remember. Now she lives in Petrograd and studies at the Smolny Institute, and is terribly happy, as she is waiting impatiently for the day when the school break ends. Well so long, goodbye my darling Papa. I squeeze and hug you very very tighly in my mind, like I love you. Your very own, Kazanetz. Regards to all. May God keep you. +

Maria (left) and Anastasia with their "Papa"

---

[99] Catherine Schneider, one of the ladies at court

Letter from Anastasia to Nicholas II

11 January, 1916. Tsarskoe Selo. My dear Papa Darling! I am still in bed, but I think tomorrow I will get up for the first time. My bronchitis is gone now. In the morning before breakfast I stay in bed in my room and write or Shura reads to me, and I go to the playroom for breakfast, and there get into bed. Mama comes for tea and sits until 6 o'cl. Yesterday Aleksei was in a very military mood, what he did not do, he was so terribly funny. Now we have nice weather, the sun comes out and not much melts, so that it is rather warm and nice. Tomorrow is a month since the 1st Hundred[100] left Mogilev. Yesterday we all wrote to Aunt Olga, as some man was going there. It's such a shame that they took your little shovel, but hope that they gave you a new one, or the same one! Mordvinov is probably charming, yes? We will soon have breakfast with Aleksei, but he will not finish very fast, while I am ready in 10 min. or faster. Mama will now sit on the balcony with Maria. "Ortipo" and "Joy" asked to send big regards and to tell you that they miss you. I am so bored sitting in bed and being unable to go to our infirmary – this is desperately boring. I send you awfully big 1000 kisses. May God keep you. Your loving loyal and faithful Kaspiyitz.

Maria's diary entries

12 January. In the morning went to Molebna, 5 with Mama. Breakfast with the same. In the afternoon rode in the troika, 3 with Isa. Had tea 4 with Mama and Anya. Rode with Shura. Had dinner 3 with Mama on the couch. Kiki, Kolya and Anya were here. It was cozy.

---

[100] Regiment

13 January. In the morning had history, and Batushka, and French reading lessons. Had breakfast with A[nastasia], Al[eksei] and Mama on the couch. In the afternoon walked along Mama's equipage. Went to our infirmary. Had tea with Mama, A., and Anya. Had a music [lesson], did homework. Dinner 4 with Mama on the couch. Anya was here.

21 January. Had lessons in the morning. Breakfast 4 with Papa and Mama on the couch. In the afternoon went to our infirmary with A., Gerashenevsky had surgery. Walked with T. and A. Had tea 4 with Mama, Papa and Sonia Dehn[101]. There was music. Did homework. Dinner 3 with Papa and Mama on the couch. Anya was here, Papa read.

27 January. Had lessons in the morning. Breakfast 5 with Papa and Mama on the couch. Went to Petrograd with Papa, to the Winter Palace infirmary for 450 lower ranks. Had tea at Grandmama's with Uncle Mimi[102]. Returned. Had a French lesson. Had dinner with Papa, Uncle Mimi and Mama on the couch. Anya was here.

1 February. Had lessons in the morning. Rode with Shura. Breakfast 5 with Mama on the couch. Went to our infirmary with A. Rode in the troika with Nastenka. Had tea 4 with Mama and Anya. Went 5 to Vsenoshnaya. Had dinner and Mama on the couch. Anya was here.

Letter from Maria to Nicholas II

---

[101] Lili Dehn's sister in law, Sofia Vladimirovna, nee Sheremetieva.

[102] Again, Grand Duke Michael Alexandrovich.

2 February. My dear Papa! I just returned from Obednya, I was at the lower church with Tatiana, as she now went to change dressings. And Olga, Anastasia and Aleksei are going to church now. Mama is in bed, her cheek hurts terribly. I don't know what we will do today, probably nothing special. Anya wanted to invite us, with Irina Tolstaya, but Irina is playing the balalaika somewhere today. I am sure that Nikolai Dmitrievich[103] will go to the upper church, because I will not be there, and I am angry in advance. I have not seen him for more than three weeks now. Tomorrow the sisters are going to Petrograd to accept charities. Today we need to go to the Grand Palace as we have not been [there] for two days already. I don't really know what to do before breakfast. Everyone is at church, so [there is] no one to walk or ride with. Maybe Mama will let me walk alone, I will go ask her. Well, so long, goodbye, my darling. I mentally squeeze you tightly in a hug and kiss you. Your Kazanetz. May God keep you. + Regards to all.

---

[103] Again Demenkov

"Your Kazanetz". Maria in her regiment's uniform.

Maria's diary entries

2 February. Went to the lower church for Obednya with T. Breakfast 5. Mama was in bed all day with a tooth abscess. In the afternoon 4 went to the G.[rand] P.[alace]. Rode

in the troika with Nastenka. Had tea 4 with Mama and Anya. Rode with T., A. and Shura. Had dinner 4, Mama was lying on the couch for a bit. Anya was here.

3 February. Had lessons in the morning. Breakfast 5 and Mama on the couch. Went to our infirmary with Anya. Rode with A. and Shura. Had tea with Mama and A. and Anya. Did homework. Had a French reading [lesson]. Had dinner 4 with Mama on the couch. Anya was here. Our [army] took [the town of] Erzerum[104].

5 February. Had lessons. Rode with Shura. Breakfast 4 and Mama on the couch. Al. was in bed all day. Went to a concert at our infirmary with A.[nastasia]. Morfesi was there and also Sasha Makarov[105] and De Lazari played the guitar. One of them played the accordion. In the afternoon had tea 4 with Mama and Anya. Rode with O., T. and Shura. Had a music [lesson]. Had dinner 4 with Mama in the playroom. Anya was here.

9 February. Had lessons in the morning. Breakfast 4 with Papa, and Mama on the couch. Had a lesson in the afternoon. Went 4 to the Grand Palace. Rode in the troika 4 with Isa. Had tea 4 with Mama and Anya. Had a music [lesson]. Went to Zhylik's[106] concert at the gymnasium. Had dinner 4 with Papa, and Mama on the couch. Anya was here. Pasted in the album[107] with Papa.

Letter from Anastasia to Nicholas II

---

[104] She is referring to the war news

[105] Alexander Makarov- Senator and Minister of Internal Affairs

[106] M. Gilliard's nickname

[107] She is referring to pasting photographs into a photo album

15 February, 1916. Tsarskoe Selo. My Precious Papa Darling. It is so pleasant that the sun came out today, it has not been out for a long time. Yesterday we three little ones, so to speak, went to Anya's infirmary where they had a concert. It was really nice. One little 10 year old girl danced the Russian [dance] with an accordion, it was so sweet, and I felt sorry for her. Delazari and Yu. Morfesi, Sasha Makarov and your friend Lersky were there as usual. He talked about an art lesson, it was so incredibly funny that the soldiers were crying from laughter. Then he talked about how you can hear the piano being played on three floors, also rather funny, and finally about the zoo, how they explain all the animals, etc. Nikolai Dmitrievich was also there, and Irina Tolstaya. While Olga and Tatiana were at their infirmary at this time, and they also had a concert. Fersen Bezobrazov and various young ladies played the balalaikas there, and many others. So you think we are not going to [another] concert, right? You are mistaken, we are going to the Grand Palace, where they will have something like a comedy of the crooked mirror, so we are going there as they begged us desperately. "Sleep the achievement of pride, everyone sleep." Now I will have the arithmetic lesson. Maria and Aleksei have colds and they don't go out except to the infirmaries. Well I will end. I send you an awfully big kiss. Regards to yours. Your loving loyal and faithful Kaspiyitz.

Maria's diary entries

20 February. Rode with A. and Shura. Walked-skipped with A. Breakfast 5 with Papa and Mama and 2 Englishmen. In the afternoon built the tower[108] 4 with Papa and the sailors. Went to our infirmary with A. Sat with Sh.[akh]-N.[Nazarov]. Had tea with Papa,

---

[108] Snow tower they built in the Alexander Park

Mama and Uncle Pavel. Went to Vsenoshnaya 4 with Papa. Had dinner with the same with Mama on the couch. Papa read, Anya was here.

21 February – Sunday. In the morning went to Obednya 5 with Papa. Breakfast with same, Mordvinov and Mama on the couch. 4 went to the Grand Palace. Walked, built the tower 4 with Papa and Mordvinov. Had tea 4 with Papa and Mama. Saw a cinematograph in English. Dinner 4 with Papa, Mordvinov and Mama on the couch. Papa read. Anya was here.

22 February. Had lessons. Then went to church 5 with Papa. Breakfast with same, with Vikitsky and Mama on the couch. In the afternoon went to our infirmary with A. Sat with Sh.N.[109] Walked 5 with Papa, built and jumped off the tower. Had tea in the playroom. Had an English lesson. Went to church 5 with Papa and Mama. Had dinner with same except Al. Papa read, Anya was here.

23 February. Had lessons. Went to church 5 with Papa. Breakfast with same, with Count Sheremetiev and Mama on the couch. Built the tower, and jumped from it. Had tea in the playroom. Had music. Went to church 5 with Papa and Mama. Had dinner 4 with Papa, Count Sheremetiev and Mama on the couch. Papa read, Anya was here.

---

[109] Shakh-Nazarov, the patient mentioned earlier

"Built the tower and jumped from it"

24 February. Had lessons in the morning. Went to church 5 with Papa. Breakfast with same, with Kazakevich and Mama on the couch. In the afternoon went to our infirmary with A. This husband and wife [couple] were there, sat with M.Z.G. and A.V.K. Built the tower. Had tea with Papa, Mama, O., A., and Alek. [sei]. Went to church 5 with Papa and Mama. Dinner with same except Al.[eksei]. Grigori and Anya were here.

25 February. Lessons as usual. Went to church 5 with Papa. Breakfast with same and Mama on the couch. Built the tower. Went to our infirmary with A., sat with Sh.N. Had tea with Papa, Mama and O. and A. Went to church 5 with Papa and Mama. Had dinner with same except Al. Papa read. Anya was here.

26 February - Friday. Had lessons. Then to church 4 with Mama. Breakfast 5 with Mama on the couch. Went to the Grand Palace with A. Built the tower. Had tea 4 with

Papa and Mama. Confessed. Went to church 5 with Papa and Mama. Had dinner 4 with Papa, Silaev and Mama on the couch.

27 February – Saturday. Received communion with the entire family. Then had tea. Rode in a troika 4 with Isa. Breakfast 5 with Papa, Count Fredericks[110], and Mama on the couch. In the afternoon went to our infirmary with A. Sat with Sh.N. Built the tower. Had tea 4 with Papa and Mama. Went 4 to Vsenoshnaya. Dinner 4 with Papa and Mama on the couch. Anya was here.

28 February. Went to Obednya 5 with Papa and Mama, breakfast with same and Kashin. Rode in the troika 4 with Isa. Walked. Had tea with Papa, Mama and Dmitri. Saw a cinematograph about the French war. Rode 4 with Shura. Dinner 4 with Papa and Mama on the couch. Papa read "In White Raiment"[111]. Anya was here.

29 February. Had lessons. Breakfast 5 with Papa, Uncle Georgi[112] and Ioann[113]. In the afternoon went to our infirmary with A. Sat with M.Z. Baron, Ton, and A.V. Walked and built the tower. Had tea with A. and T. in the playroom. Had English and music lessons. Did homework. Dinner 3 with Papa, Ioann and Dmitri. Papa read, Anya was here. Mama has neuralgia, and she stayed in bed almost the entire day.

2 March. Had lessons. Saw Papa off. Went to the cemetery with A. and T., got stuck in the snow, and there was so much snow at the cemetery that we sunk almost to our

---

[110] Count Vladimir Borisovich Fredericks – Imperial Household Manager

[111] By William Le Queux

[112] Grand Duke Georgi Mikhailovich

[113] Prince Ioann Konstantinovich

waist. Breakfast 5. Rode in the troika with Isa, went to the tower. Had tea 4 with Mama and Anya. Had music and French lessons. Before tea went to our infirmary with A., sat with everyone. M.Z. sat. Dinner 3 and Mama on the couch. Anya was here.

Letter from Maria to Nicholas II

3 March. My sweet and dear Papa! Yesterday after we saw you off, Tatiana, Anastasia and I went to the cemetery in a motor. We drove there for an unusually long time because the roads are so bad. We arrived there and went to the officers' graves, there was nothing there yet, and too much snow, then I wanted to visit the graves of our patients from the lower ranks. There was a big pile of snow on the side of the road, so I was able to climb up with great difficulty on my knees and jump down from it. Down there the snow turned out to be above the knees, and although I was wearing long boots, I was already wet so I decided to continue ahead. Nearby I found one grave with the surname Mishenko, this was the name of our patient; I laid down some flowers there and walked ahead, and suddenly I saw the same surname again, I looked up at the board, [to see] which regiment he was from, and it turned out that he was one of our patients [too], but not the same one. So I laid down the flowers for him and was just starting to walk away when I fell on my back, and was lying there for almost a minute not knowing how to get up, there was so much snow that I could not reach the ground with my hand for leverage. I finally got up and walked ahead. Earlier Tatiana and Anastasia said that they were going to go to another cemetery, to Sonia Orbeliani [grave] and that they will return for me. But instead they sent the man in charge of the graveyard to help me. He crawled over to me with great difficulty and we went to look for another grave together. We searched and searched and could not understand at all

what happened to it. It turned out that it was closer to the fence and that we should have climbed over a ditch. He stood in the ditch and said to me "I will carry you over", I said "no", he said "let's try". Of course he put me down not on the other side but right in the middle of the ditch. And so we are both standing in the ditch, up to our bellies in snow, and dying from laughter. It was hard for him to climb out, as the ditch was deep, and for me too. So he climbed out somehow and stretched his hands out to me. Of course I slid back down into the ditch on my stomach about three times, but finally climbed out. And we performed all this with flowers in our hands. Then we couldn't fit through between the crosses for a while, as we were both wearing our coats. But in the end I did find the grave. Finally we were able to leave the cemetery. Tatiana and Anastasia were already waiting for me on the road. I felt half-dead from heat and dampness. We climbed into the motors and drove away. I took off one boot to shake out the snow. At this same time we ran into a wagon. We were driving rather fast. We just swerved to the side a little, when Lapin's steering wheel spun [out of control] and our front tires slid into a snow bank, and scarily [we] turned to our side, I jumped out wearing one boot and put the other one back on out on the road. What could we do, no one was there anymore and it was already 1 o'clock 10 minutes. Then we 3 decided to walk home on foot, but luckily at this moment some squadron was walking back from shooting practice and they dug out the motor, while we walked almost all the way to the shooting gallery. The motor caught up to us and we got home safely. But the road was so bad the entire time that we were certain that the motor would break. Across from the Cuirassier Cathedral. And we were tossed up so high that Tatiana almost hit her head on the roof. In the afternoon during our troika ride we almost ran over another sleigh. So after all this, we went to our infirmary, and we were certain that we will fall into a ditch or something else will happen to us again. [We] went to the tower yesterday. The sailors were all very sweet and worked hard. You were very much missed there. […]   In the evening Anya finished reading "Our People Abroad" to us. Olga went to bed early of course. And you are probably enjoying the English book. Grandmama sent the book "Olive", and Mama sent her another one. Well, farewell my darling. May Christ be with you. + Your Kazanetz. I kiss you affectionately and squeeze you a lot and for a long time. Titanis titanis. Dukchik Dukchik[114].

Letters from Anastasia to Nicholas II

5 March, 1916. T.S. [and] 6 March. My precious Papa Darling. Well I am sending you the pictures I took which you wanted. Olga and I did not go to the tower, but Tatiana and Maria went there and tell us that it's really nice now. […]. We ride in the troika, which is pleasant, but because everything is starting to melt, big pieces [of ice] end up in one's physiognomy, and it hurts terribly, but I bear this pain. Mama is reading your letter to us, which she got today. We just returned from church and already had dinner. Maria asked me to tell you that the tower is very nice and that they poured some putrid water from the small pond, the one near the tower, on the gangway today. That Sidor[115] was very funny and ordered her around, where and how she should work. Fedotov does not forget his responsibilities either and was ordering everyone around. Right now it is foggy, but not too heavy. Well, farewell for now, until tomorrow.

---

[114] Appears to be some private language with her "Papa".

[115] One of the sailors

6 March. Well I greet you with a good morning. We already went to church and had breakfast with Isa too. And now Von Nerik, a commander from my regiment was here to [see] me. His face is most simple, not very German as a face. He said that the regiment is stationed in the same spot, and right now he is in reserves only for 12 days, and then they will sit in the trenches for 12 days, but still every day about 10 or more lower ranks are wounded, but very few officers, so all is well. We will now go to the Grand Palace, this is not fun, and they will go riding, and then to Anya's, and a magician will be there, a very good one I think. Well I must go get dressed. I give you an awfully huge kiss. Regards to all yours. Your loving loyal and faithful Kaspiyitz. May God keep you. Sleep well.

Maria's diary entry

7 March. Had lessons. Rode with Shura, breakfast 5, with Mama on the couch. Went to our infirmary with A. Ivan bid farewell to us as he is leaving from the Svodny regiment and returning to the Black Sea. Went to Vitebsk community infirmary with Isa, in the barracks of the 3rd St. Regiment. Had tea 4 with Mama and Anya. Had English and music lessons. Rode in a troika with O., A. and Shura. Had dinner 4 and Mama on the couch. Lili Dehn[116] with [her] husband, Anya and Baron Taube were here. Sat and looked at a [photo] album, then went to tea. It was very cozy.

---

[116] Wife of a naval officer and friend of the imperial family.

Left to right: Maria, Olga, Anastasia and Tatiana during a ride in the snow.

Letters from Maria to Nicholas II

9 March. My dear darling Papa! Today is Spring already, but it's 7 [degrees] below here and snow with wind. Completely unacceptable. [I] just finished breakfast. Olga and Tatiana are going to Petrograd for charities and committee, and will have tea at Grandmama's, and will also stop by Aunt Ksenia's[117] who feels terrible and does not leave the house. I will now go to our infirmary with A. Nikolai Dmitrievich bade farewell to Mama. Before that, the regiment had a goodbye party for him in the evening at 7 o'clock, which only ended at 5 in the morning, so Resin looked rather sad, and when he

---
[117] Grand Duchess Ksenia Alexandrovna, the Tsar's sister

was leaving the room [he] almost knocked over a vase with flowers, and his voice was not very nice either. But N.D. himself was very charming. I have not seen him since then, and don't even expect to anymore. Right now Anastasia is sitting here and playing the balalaika. Well so long, my dear. I kiss you affectionately and apologize for a boring letter. Your Kazanetz. May Christ be with you. +

14 March. My precious Papa! Oh well, Nikolai Dmitrievich left on Saturday. I spoke with him on the telephone. He was awfully happy to be leaving. Do you remember I sewed him a shirt, so I asked him, and he said that it fits him very well. Yesterday 3 medical trains arrived here, one of them is mine, and we went there and saw about 300 soldiers and 8 officers. I am writing to you from Orchie's[118] room. Mama is lying on the couch, and Vladimir Nikolaevich[119] is doing electrotherapy on her. I just rode around with Shura. Igor[120] will have breakfast with us. In the afternoon I will go to our infirmary with Anastasia. They haven't brought the wounded there yet, but I think [they are] supposed to on Sunday. Yesterday Voikov[121] was at church and from afar he looks a bit like Nikolai Dmitrievich, what swine, how dare he. And instead of Popov, I think Voronov will be in the regiment, as he is not completely healthy and needs to do something with his throat. We are really not doing anything interesting at all. When we have time, [we] ride around with Shura before dinner. It is so strange that it's still rather light outside at 6

---

[118] Mrs Mary Ann Orchard, the governess

[119] Vladimir Nikolaevich Derevenko, the imperial physician

[120] Prince Igor Konstantinovich.

[121] General- Major and Commandant of the Imperial Court

o'clock. Well, farewell for now, my dear. I love you very very much, squeeze and kiss you. Your very own Kazanetz. May the Lord keep you. + Regards to all.

Maria's diary entries

20 March. Went to church with Papa and Mama. Had breakfast 5, Papa and Mama on the couch. 4 went to the Gr.[and] Pal.[ace]. Walked with Papa and Mama [rode] in an equipage. Broke the ice 4 with Papa. Had tea in the playroom. 5 went to Anya's concert at the infirmary, "Ivanov Pavel" and the magicians. Went to our infirmaries with A., 17 soldiers arrived from the train. Rode with A. and Shura. Had dinner 5 with Papa, Mama, Silaev and Anya. Papa read.

26 March. Walked with Trina, had lessons, rode with Shura. Had breakfast 5 with Papa and Mama, Count Fredericks, and Count Kutaisov. Broke the ice with Papa and the sailors. Mama was there. Papa departed, [we] saw him and Dmitri off. Had tea 4 and Mama. Went to Vsenoshnoya 5 with Mama. Had dinner 4 and Mama on the couch. Anya was here.

27 March. Sunday. Went to Church 5 with Mama, breakfast with same and Isa. Went to our infirmary with A. Rode 4 with Mama and Anya. Went to a concert at Anya's infirmary 5 with Mama. Rode 2 with Shura. Had dinner 4 and Mama on the couch. Anya was here.

Olga, Nicholas and Maria: "We go outside and break the ice." One of the Tsar's and his daughters' favorite activities during winter months was breaking the ice on Alexander Park canals.

Letter from Anastasia to Nicholas II

31 March, 1916. T.S. My precious Papa Darling. I am hurrying to write to you as we must go to the infirmary. Maria and I and Aleksei had breakfast upstairs as Mama and the sisters are in Petrograd. We go outside and break the ice. Yesterday Fedotov was not there. Krylov is terribly weak and showed up. Maria and I are now playing, she on the piano, and I on the balalaika, and it's turning out rather well, but it's even better with Olga. I imagine how the 1st Hundred was happy to see you there in particular and I was a little envious of you. We will go break the ice again today, and to two infirmaries, to

ours and the Grand Palace. I give you a terribly big kiss and squeeze you. Your loving loyal and faithful Kaspiyitz. +

Maria's diary entries

3 April. Went to church 5 with Mama, Aunt Olga and Christo[122] and had breakfast. Went 4 to the Gr.[and] Pal.[alace]. Rode with Mama and Anya. Went to our infirmary. Had tea with Mama and Dmitri. Rode with Shura. Had dinner 4 and Mama on the couch. Anya was here. Read.

4 April. Monday. Walked with Trina. Went to church 5 with Mama, breakfast with same. Rode 4 with Isa. Went to our infirmary with A., then went to [see] the construction of the new infirmary with Loman and Ev.[geni] Al.[ekseevich] Had tea 4 with Mama and Anya. Went to church 5 with Mama. Had dinner 4 and Mama on the couch. Anya was here. Read.

5 April, Tuesday. Rode with Shura. Went to church with Mama, had breakfast with same and Uncle Petya. Rode 4 with Isa. Went to our infirmary with A. [...] Had tea 4 with Mama and Anya. Went to church 5 with Mama. Had dinner 4 and Mama on the couch. Anya was here - read again.

6 April, Wednesday. Aleksei's arm hurts, sat with him with A. at 5 in the morning. Went to the Gr. Pal. With A. Then went to church 4 with Mama, breakfast with same. Rode 4 with Trina, went to our infirmary with A. Went to look at the radiology machine, Loman's

---

[122] The son of Queen Olga of Greece

chancellery and again to the construction [site]. Had tea and went to church 4 with Mama. Had dinner with same with Anya. Confessed before Vsenoshnaya.

Letter from Maria to Nicholas II

7 April, Thursday. My darling sweet Papa! I ask for your forgiveness before confession. Olga wanted to send you a telegram for this occasion yesterday, but of course forgot. It was so sad to have communion without you and Aleksei. The weather now is wonderful here. In the morning when we were driving to church it was foggy, but now it is wonderfully sunny and the sky is blue. Just finished breakfast and [we] will now go riding with Mama and Anya. We had breakfast upstairs in the playroom near Aleksei. His arm is not hurting now. A lot of soldiers and Cossacks were at communion today, awfully appetizing hetmans. Of course Batushka's entire family was there. It's such a shame that you did not have communion at Stavka[123]. Well, I must end. May Christ be with you. I kiss you affectionately. Your Kazanetz.

---

[123] Russian Military Headquarters in Mogilev

"A lot of soldiers and Cossacks were at communion today, awfully appetizing hetmans." Maria and Aleksei with Cossacks.

Maria's diary entries

7 April – Thursday. Received communion 4 with Mama, while Al. [did] later, [his] arm was hurting. Had tea all together. Rode 4 with Isa. Had breakfast 4 with Mama, while Al. [was] in bed. Rode 4 with Mama with Anya. Went to our infirmary with A. Had tea 4 with Mama and Anya. Went to 12 Gospels 4 with Mama, and had dinner with same. Anya was here.

8 April – Friday. Rode with Anya and Shura. Went to our infirmary with A., sat with the sisters. Had breakfast 4 with Mama near Al. Went to the Shroud Procession[124] 4 with Mama. Had tea 4 with Mama and Anya. Played 4 with Zhylik. Went 4 with Mama to the Burial[125]. Had dinner with same near Al. Anya was here. Made drawings.

9 April. Went to our infirmary with A. Went to church 4 with Mama. Had breakfast 5 and Mama on the couch, with Mama and Anya. Had tea with same and Kolya. Rode with A. and Shura. Had dinner 4 with Mama on the couch. Went to zautrennya[126] 5 with Mama and had dinner. Broke the fast with Mama and Anya.

Letter from Anastasia to Nicholas II

9 April, 1916. Tsarskoe Selo. Indeed He Has Risen! Huge thanks to you, my precious Papa Darling for the picture and the very appetizing egg. I wish you all the very very best. I also thank you for the flowers which we got yesterday, I love them so much, they are called "prosurenchiki". I miss you so terribly much, that you are not here with us, but at least those who are with you must be very happy to have you near them. Regards to all. I give you a terribly big triple kiss, and many little ones to your hand and cheek and everywhere. Your loving loyal and faithful always and everywhere. Kaspiyitz. May God keep you.

Maria's diary entries

---

[124] Easter ceremony

[125] Easter ceremony

[126] Early morning prayer service

10 April – Sunday. Easter Christ's Resurrection. Went to Khristovanie[127] with Mama. Had breakfast with same. Went to our infirmary with A. Exchanged Easter greetings with everyone. Then went to the Palace infirmary 4 with Mama and sat in the parlor. Had tea 4 with Mama and Anya. Rode with A. and Shura. Went 4 to church. Had dinner with same and Mama on the couch. Anya was here.

11 April. Went 4 to Obednya and the Procession of the Cross[128]. Had breakfast 5 and Mama on the couch. The same went to Khristovanie at the Gr. Pal. infirmary, and upstairs for the officers and soldiers. Went to our infirmary with A. Had tea 4 with Mama and Anya. Aleksei showed a cinematograph, rode 4 with Shura. Had dinner 4 with Mama on the couch. Anya was here.

Maria's diary entries

12 April. Went on Olga's train with A., O. and Isa. Walked with A. and Isa. Went to our infirmary with A. and sat outside in fresh air. Had breakfast 5 and Mama on the couch. Went 4 with Mama to Khristovanie at Matveyevsky infirmary and the Red Cross. Had tea with same and Dmitri. Everyone went to a concert at Anya's infirmary. Yu. Morfessi, Sasha Makarov and DeLazari, Orlov, etc. were there. Rode in the evening and the afternoon 4 with Nastenka. Had dinner 4 and Mama on the couch. Anya was here.

---

[127] Easter greetings

[128] Easter ceremony

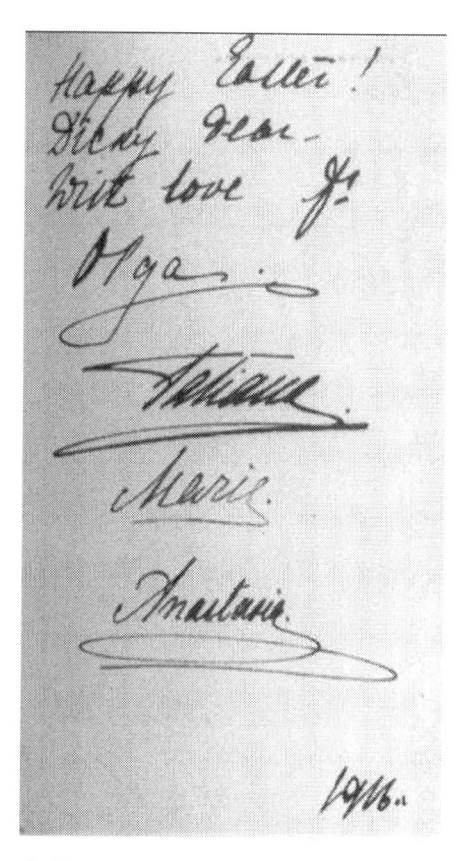

Easter card from the Romanov sisters to their cousin "Dicky" Mountbatten in England.

15 April. Walked with O., A. and Trina. Went to our infirmary with A., sat outside. Went to the cemetery with Mama, A. and Anya. Breakfast 5 with Papa and Mama and Vilkin. Walked 4 with Papa, while Mama and Anya rode. Had tea in Pavlovsk with Aunt Olga, Christo, Aunt Mavra, Elena[129], Ioannchik, Igor, Vera, and Georgi. Rode with Trina, A. and Isa, while Al. behind us with Zhylik. Had dinner 4 with Papa and Mama on the couch. Papa read. Anya was here.

---

[129] Wife of Prince Ioann.

16 April. Walked with O., A. and Trina, later went to the Gr. Pal. with A. and to our infirmary. Had breakfast 5 with Papa, Mama, Uncle Georgi, and Count Fredericks, Count Sheremetiev. Walked 4 with Papa and Mama [rode] in an equipage. [They] went in row boats for the first time, I [was] in a kayak. Had tea with Papa and Mama, and same were in church and had dinner with Count Sheremetiev. Saw the Apraksins[130] with [their] 3 children. Papa read. Anya was here.

17 April. Went to Obednya 4 with Papa and Mama. Had breakfast 5 with Papa, Mama and Dmitri and Silaev. Walked 4 with Papa and Mama and Anya in an equipage. Went to the wedding of An.P.[131] with A. and Nastenka. She married Ivanov – an officer from the Primorsky regiment. Had tea 4 with Papa, Mama. Rode 4 with Nastenka. Had dinner 4 with Papa, Mama, Kolya Silaev and Anya.

18 April. Had lessons. Picked up Aunt Ella. Breakfast 5 with Papa, Mama and Aunt Ella. In the afternoon went to our infirmary with A., went to the construction [site]. Rode bicycles with Papa and A. while Al. and T. [rode] in a small motor. Had tea with T. and A. in the playroom. Had two lessons. Rode with A. and Trina. Had dinner 3 with Papa, Aunt.

19 April. Had lessons in the morning. Walked with Trina. Had breakfast 5 with Papa, Mama and Aunt Ella. Same went to the cemetery, panikhida for all the [deceased] soldiers. Walked 4 with Papa, and then sailed around in row boats. Had tea with Papa,

---

[130] One of the Russian noble families

[131] Anna Pavlovna

Mama, Aunt Ella and O. Singing lesson. Rode [with] A. and Shura. Had dinner 3 with Papa, Mama and Aunt Ella, Dmitri. Anya was here. Papa finished reading the book.

23 April. Went to church 5 with Papa and Mama. Had breakfast with the entire family. Rode bicycles 4 with Papa, then in row boats. Had tea 4 with Papa and Mama on the balcony. Went to church 4 with Papa. Had dinner with same with Maslov and Mama. Grigori was here. Rode 4 with Papa and Mama in a motor. Anya was here.

24 April. Went to Obednya 4 with Papa and Mama. Breakfast 5 with Papa, Mama and Sandro. Walked 4 with Papa. Saw Papa off. He went to Stavka[132] in Mogilev. Went to our infirmary. Walked around the construction site with the officers. Had tea 4 with Mama and Anya on the balcony. Rode 4 with Nastenka. Had dinner 4 with Mama on the balcony, rode in a motor. Anya was here.

25 April. Had lessons. Rode with Shura. Had breakfast 5 with Anya and Mama on the couch. Went 4 to the Gr. Pal. Went to our infirmary with A. Then to the Convoy barracks infirmary. Had tea 4 with Mama on the balcony. Had lessons. Rode with A. and Trina. Had dinner 4 with Mama, Kiki and Kolya. Sat and watched the soldiers play checkers. Anya was here. Kiki and Kolya left for the front.

28 April. Had lessons. Went to our infirmary with A. Had breakfast 5 with Mama on the couch. Drove 4 with Mama to Petrograd to the English infirmary and one at Dmitri's palace. Had tea at Grandmama's with Aunt Ksenia. Returned with A. and Trina. Had dinner 4 with Mama on the couch. Read.

---

[132] The Tsar's military headquarters

5 May[133]. Walked around at the [train] stations. Breakfast 4 with Isa, Resin, Zolotarev, Zhylik, V. N. and 2 engineers. Arrived in Mogilev. Went in motors across the Dnepr[134] 4 with Papa and Mama and the Suite, and walked. Had tea in the train with same. Went to Vsenoshnaya 4 with Papa and Mama. Had dinner at Stavka, sat with Uncle Boris[135] and

6 May. Went to church 4 with Papa and Mama. There were greetings. At breakfast sat with Uncle Kyrill[136] and Igor. In the afternoon walked on the rails 5 with Papa. Had tea in the train. Everyone went to [see] a cinematograph. At dinner sat with Uncle Sergei[137] and Uncle Boris. Returned to the train.

7 May. Walked around the [train] station. Wrote. At breakfast sat with Uncle Kyrill and Igor. Walked, saw 1 Battalion. Left Mogilev. Everyone had tea with the Suite. Played ball with A. At dinner sat with Nilov and Igor. After tea saw 2 Battalions at the station.

15 May. Sat on the deck at the pier. Went to Obednya at the Vladimirsky Cathedral, then went to see a panorama. At breakfast sat with Grigorovich and Nilov. Went to the Georgievsky Monastery and reviewed forts on the way, also went to the Church of Ioann the Warrior[138]. Had tea. Ioann and Mikhail (Kolya's brother) were here. At tea sat with Grigorovich. Played like yesterday. Had tea.

---

[133] They were on their way to visit Nicholas and Aleksei at Stavka

[134] River

[135] Grand Duke Boris Vladimirovich

[136] Grand Duke Kyrill Vladimirovich

[137] Grand Duke Sergei Mikhailovich

[138] Christian saint, aka "John the Warrior".

25 May. Went to Obednya with Mama. Had breakfast with same on the balcony. Went to your infirmary with A. Rode 4 with Nastenka. Had tea 4 on the balcony with Mama, Aunt Olga, Aunt Mavra[139] and Aunt Michen[140]. Drove 4 with Mama to Anya's house, where we saw Grigori and Munika[141]. Had dinner 4 with Mama. Went to the sisters' infirmary, put together a puzzle with Grekova, the Countess, Natarovich, Nikiforov, Karankozov and the Doctor.

Maria, Olga and Tatiana in front of the imperial train. Most likely Anastasia took this photo.

---

[139] Grand Duchess Elizaveta Mavrikievna

[140] Grand Duchess Maria Pavlovna the Elder, wife of Grand Duke Vladimir

[141] Maria "Munya" Golovina, one of court ladies and Rasputin's followers.

Letter from Anastasia to Nicholas II

27 May, 1916. T.S. My dear Papa Darling! I will soon send you the pictures that I took in Mogilev and Sevastopol, if you want them! Yesterday when I was riding around, a long distance passenger train passed by and suddenly I saw through the window a protective cherkeska[142] a red beshmet[143] and papakha[144], and further in the window a grey cherkeska and I thought I recognized Count Grabbe[145] and his Cossack, and then during the day we ran into Voikov, he was riding in a motor. Tell Aleksei that I plan to write to him, but never have time. We now pick flowers, the lilac is here already but not that much of it. The weather is not great, it rains daily nevertheless we still have breakfast and tea on the balcony. Right now I don't have a lesson and therefore I can write. Have you heard anything about the 1st Hundred! They probably have enough to do now and they are rather happy. Sometimes a Hundred comes by here for practice and returns with zurna[146], so of course we eyeball [them] and yesterday they passed by and I watched. It's a shame there are too many bushes so they can't see us well, but the important thing of course is that we can see them. We will now accompany the sisters to their inifirmary and ride back for our lessons. Everyone gives you a big kiss and Aleksei too. Your loving loyal and faithful little Kaspiyitz. May God keep you!

Letter from Maria to Nicholas II

---

[142] Type of coat

[143] A coat generally worn by people from North Caucasus or Kuban Cossacks.

[144] A type of hat

[145] General Count Alexander Grabbe

[146] Type of flute

29 May. [At] The Feodorovsky Cathedral Imperial infirmary for the Wounded. My dear Papa! I don't think I ever wrote to you on this paper before. Today it was hot here, but now [it is] not that [hot], as it rained a little. In the morning we went to Obednya and had breakfast on the balcony, also had tea with Zizi[147]. She is leaving to her village tomorrow. I am all bitten up by some nasty beast, and therefore my whole body itches. It is extremely unpleasant, especially in public, when one wants to scratch. These days we go to the sisters' infirmary almost every evening. They clean the instruments and prepare materials for the next day. Anastasia plays table croquet with the wounded, while I play bloshki[148] or put together a puzzle. This afternoon we rode around, and then went to our infirmary. Almost all the wounded are lying in the tent, only the heavily [wounded] ones are not allowed. Those who are able, walk to Catherine Park and sail around the lake in row boats. They really enjoy this and always ask the nurses to go with them. We go to our infirmary every day too, this is much better than the Grand Palace with Nurse Lyubushina. She of course noted that we got tan and all the nurses too. The other day we went to the Children's Island[149] with Poupse's[150] sister, and she weeded with us. There is so much decayed grass among the lilies of the valley that they are not growing well. We cleaned half, and will finish the other one in the next couple of days. I kiss you and Aleksei affectionately. May God keep you. + Your Kazanetz.

---

[147] Elizaveta Naryshkina- daughter of Aleksei Kurakin and Princess Yulia Golitzyna, lady in waiting.

[148] Type of game, literally translates as "little fleas".

[149] A small island in the middle of the Alexander Park, with a play house and pet cemetery, originally built by Nicholas I for his children

[150] Major-General Sergei Potosky (?)

"These days we go to the sisters' infirmary almost every evening."

Letter from Anastasia to Nicholas II

31 May, 1916. Tsarskoe Selo. We are having lessons now, but as of tomorrow we will still have lessons but not during the day anymore, and this will be very pleasant. These days Maria and I swing on giant steps a lot. We are almost never nauseous, [although] we fell a bunch of times already, but so far have not hurt ourselves. We went riding now as there is no lesson and now we are waiting for Mama and the sisters [to return] from the infirmary. We go there in the evenings and I play croquet which is sitting on a table. It is very small, but it is really fun to play. I play with 3 officers the entire evening, until they send me to bed, although most of the time I go without an invitation. Now I must finish writing as it is time to frishtyk[151] on the balcony. Today it is windy, but sunny, and somewhat warm. I listen to your and Aleksei's letters with great appetite during

---

[151] Possibly a Russianized German word?

zakuskis[152] or breakfast. I apologize that I am using different ink, but I am writing in Mama's room. Well now! I give awfully big kisses to your sweet little cheeks and hands, and Aleksei. May God keep you. Your loving loyal and faithful 14-year-old Kaspiyitz.

"Now I must finish writing as it is time to frishtyk on the balcony." Anastasia on the Alexander Palace balcony.

Maria's diary entries

---

[152] Type of appetizers between meals

1 June. Had lessons. Russian, music, English and Batushka. Went to the cemetery for Sonia's panikhida with Mama. Had breakfast 4 with Mama on the balcony. Went to our infirmary with A., Rimma Zborovskaya[153] came over, Vikt. Erastovich was wounded. Rode with Mama. Had tea with Mama, and A. and Anya. Rode with A. and Trina. Had dinner 4 with Mama. Went to the sisters' infirmary, played bloshki.

Letter from Maria to Nicholas II

4 June. My precious Papa darling! I send you good wishes for Anastasia's birthday. I am writing you on this paper, as this is the last of it from our infirmary. If you would like, I can write to you on the infirmary postcards. It is raining every day here, but despite that we still walk and ride. Yesterday morning we had lessons, but only for an hour, so Shvybz and I were free and went riding with Trina. On the way we ran into an old woman who was selling lilies of the valley, and so we bought some from her. Had breakfast on the balcony although it was not really warm. Then we went to the Grand Palace. We planned on going riding afterwards, but it was raining very hard, so we didn't go. Shvybz and I went to our infirmary. Had tea on the balcony too then swung in the hammock. It is hanging between two trees behind the path by the balcony. The trees there are very strong. You probably heard that Viktor Erastovich and Skvortzov were wounded, while Shvedov has typhus. I am writing to you in the morning, as I have a free hour. At 10 o'clock I will accompany the sisters and Mama to the infirmary. She seems to feel better, and she now goes to the infirmary earlier with the sisters. I am

---

[153] Viktor Erastovich's wife (?)

sending you, Aleksei and the Suite a few pictures. I signed all of them, but not yours. I kiss you affectionately, like I love you. Your Kazanetz, may Christ be with you. +

Maria "Had tea on the balcony..."

Letter from Anastasia to Nicholas II

5 June, 1916[154]. Tsarskoe Selo. My Precious Papa Darling! I thank you so terribly much for the long letter and all the wonderful gifts. I am sending you the cards with the angels,

---
[154] Anastasia's 15th birthday

give them to everyone to whom I signed in the back, and those that are not signed, keep them if you want. The weather is rotten and cold, and it is raining ocassionally. We just finished breakfast, and now I am sitting here and responding to telegrams, and then we will go riding, I think. We also heard about Viktor Erastovich and they told us that he was wounded in his chest, through to his back. Mama's medical train went to get them as Mama wrote to them, [asking] that if possible to get him and Skvortzov, who was slightly wounded, and bring them here. I got a telegram from Igor, today is his name day. I got a small brooch, a medallion and Mama's old bracelet, silver and very appetizing. Regrettably I must end as Isa, Trina and Nastenka are coming over to congratulate me, and so I have to be there. I thank you again hugely for everything. I send you a 1000000 big big kisses. Your loving loyal and faithful Kaspiyitz. 15-year old.

To Her Imperial Highness Grand Duchess Anastasia Nikolaevna For Her Birthday

Today is Anastasia's Day

And we would like for all the love and affection of entire Russia

To reach you through us

What joy it is to bring you wishes

Your best image from our dreams

And modestly sign our names

Underneath these congratulatory verses

Forgetting that just recently

We were in violent battles

We will celebrate this Fifth of June holiday in our hearts

And we will take with us to a new fight

Our hearts full of admiration

Remembering our meetings

In a palace at Tsarskoe Selo

[Signed] Ensign Gumilev[155]

5 June, 1916, Tsarskoe Selo

The Grand Palace Infirmary

Maria and Anastasia with their wounded

---

[155] Nikolai Stepanovich Gumilev: Ensign of the 5th Hussar Alexandriysky Regiment, patient at the Grand Paalce Infirmary

Maria's diary entry

5 June. Went to Obednya 4 with Mama. Had breakfast with same and Anya. Rode 4 with Mama. Went to our infirmary with A. Had tea and dinner 4 with Mama. Sat with Nastenka and looked at albums. Went to the sisters' infirmary. Played bloshki...

Letter from Anastasia to Nicholas II

9 June. My dear Papa Darling. We just played ping pong with Maria and were bustling around and yelling so incredibly much that now my hands are shaking like someone with a head injury. I think that in a few days they will bring Viktor Erastovich to our infirmary, he requested for another cornet from the Tekinsky Regiment to come with him, they will bring them from Poltava. Of course this is pleasant. We are now moving to a nearby infirmary, the one that looks out on to the Convoy gathering and the Sobor[156]. We will have an infirmary there now, so very cozy. Maria and I went there a few times to look, and we were satisfied. Today Mama, Olga and Tatiana are going to the city for the Executive Committee, and I don't envy them, while Maria and I are staying here. We keep swinging in the hammock. Well, when Vera and Georgi were here, they had breakfast [here] with their mother[157]. So we picked them up and swung them, Vera was really happy, while Georgi was getting scared, and then Vera and Georgi started to fight, and we were instigating them a little against each other and laughing. It will probably start raining now, but of course I am not afraid of this as I am a brave little soldier. Well here is comes, congratulations!!! I wrote all the news and anything

---

[156] Feodorovsky Cathedral

[157] Grand Duchess Elizaveta Mavrikievna "Aunt Mavra", and her two youngest children

interesting, and the rest is the usual. Well, I will end my silly message now, masses of kisses to you and Aleksei. May Christ be with you. Regards to all of yours. Miss [you]. Your loving loyal and faithful little Kaspiyitz. All the sisters kiss you.

Letter from Maria to Nicholas II

12 June. My Papa precious darling! Yesterday morning we had lessons, and during the last hour Shvybz and I were free, as Zhylik is not here. We took advantage of that and went to the Grand Palace. Then, after we returned home, we waited for Mama and the sisters for breakfast until 13.30. After breakfast we went to the panikhida for Zhukov and two other Cossacks. Then we returned home. Shvybz and I waited out the rain and went to our infirmary. On the way a motor caught up to us, it was going rather fast, we moved to the side of the road in order not to be sprayed with dirt. The motor passes and who do you think is in it? Loman? Nothing of a sort, who but Viktor Erastovich himself. He was riding next to Ensign Tolstov of the Tekinsky regiment, and across from them, with her back to the driver sat the sister of mercy who brought them from Poltava in a regular train. We got to the infirmary at the same time. The motor stopped. The sister of mercy came out and helped Viktor Erastovich. He came over so pitifully to greet us that it was a bit unnecessary. Of course he was, as always, [wearing] his gray cherkeska, but [it was] very battered, his little papakha was also dirty. We greeted the nurse, she had an appetizingly tan face. "Well, I brought them to you", - she said, smiling. Tolstov was wearing his uniform, a burgundy robe and a huge black papakha. Underneath his huge papakha he looked very small, wretched and thin. He is almost the same height as Viktor Erastovich. After that we entered the infirmary and went to the lower ranks' room.

There is a woman patient there, a volunteer from my regiment. They offered her a separate room, but she did not want it, saying that she is the same soldier like everyone else. She looks like a boy, although she is 33 years old. While we were with the soldiers, Viktor Erastovich went home for 10 minutes, of course he stayed there for a half hour, because a lot of officers came over their flat. Viktor Erastovich came back to the infirmary while we were sitting in his room with Tolstov. He was tired from walking and therefore agreed to sit down right away. He told us a lot about the Hundred, and in general was the same as always. He sits hunched over as his back hurts him the most. The entry wound healed already but the exit wound on his back – did not, the bullet luckily did not touch the spine. Guess who I got a letter from? From Nikolai Dmitrievich. He sent me three pictures taken during their last landing. So terribly sweet, is it not? I squeeze you tightly, kiss and love you and Aleksei. May God keep you. + Your Kazanetz.

Letter from Nicholas II to Maria

Imperial Headquarters, 13 June, 1916. My dear Maria, I congratulate you on your 17th birthday and wish you everything that is bright and good. I regret to be away. I thank you for the letters, reading them I often laughed at your stories. I am also grateful for the photographs of which I now have so many. The old album is full, will need to order a new one soon - but [there is] never enough time to paste them. I am happy that Vikt. Erast. already arrived at your infirmary. Tell Shvybzik that I share her joy in seeing him and following him if she deigns him with it. Recently I read in a command that three officers in your Kazansky regiment received St George's crosses for past heroism and a few others got Georg. Weapons. This is good. For ten days the weather has been nasty, cold and constant rain. Finally today it is clear and warm and we will start eating in the tent again. Aleksei, Nagorny and Muravnukin are on the giant steps or we play sort of a hide-and-seek [game]. Well it is time to end. I embrace you tightly, my sweet Maria, and your sisters too. May Christ be with you. +. Your Papa.

Letter from Maria to Nicholas II

14 June. I don't know how to thank you, my precious Papa for your dear letter. Unfortunately I cannot write a lot to you as I am very busy. In the morning we went to the infirmary and dragged all the wounded over to the new infirmary[158]. We had breakfast just now and now we all must go to the consecration of the new infirmary. It is rather cozy. I kiss you and Aleksei affectionately. May God keep you. Your Kazanetz.

Letter from Anastasia to Nicholas II

16 June. My dear Papa Darling! I am writing out of turn as I did not have a chance to write because we were going to our new infirmary a lot. We already moved and it is terribly cozy. On the very first day they brought 3 officers there and 10 lower ranks, four of them seriously [wounded]. One boy, 16 years old, is also rather seriously wounded. On 14 June we had a real housewarming. We went to our infirmary 3 times, alone in the morning, in the afternoon with Mama and the sisters, and in the evening again alone, to a concert. It was very cozy, masses of people and wounded [were there]. But the funniest thing was when a 5 year old boy Vitya (the son of our former wounded, who is

---

[158] The new infirmary was set up in the Feodorovsky Gorodok.

now our banya[159] attendant), he started to dance and everyone poked him and he got going, it was terribly funny, everyone was enjoying it and was noisy and so forth, while he kept dancing calmly with his back to the public. When we were leaving, it was really cozy, as on the pink gangway they lit a lamp and there was pink light, [it was] awfully appetizing. Yesterday Count Grabbe came to [see] Vik. Erastovich and the Cossack who recently arrived wounded in his arm and hip, his name is something like Boyarkin. He is very merry and talks a lot. Now we feel sad passing by the old infirmary, the poor thing is just standing there, although there are 6 lower ranks [there] who do not get dressings and they are waiting to depart for Finland, so Maria and I go there, there are masses of workers and a lot of scattered things. Right now the weather is sunny and warm, [but I] don't know what it will be like in the afternoon. Well, I must end. I send [you] a terribly big kiss, Darling Papa and Aleksei 100000000 times. May God keep you, your loving loyal and faithful Kaspiyitz.

---

[159] Steam room

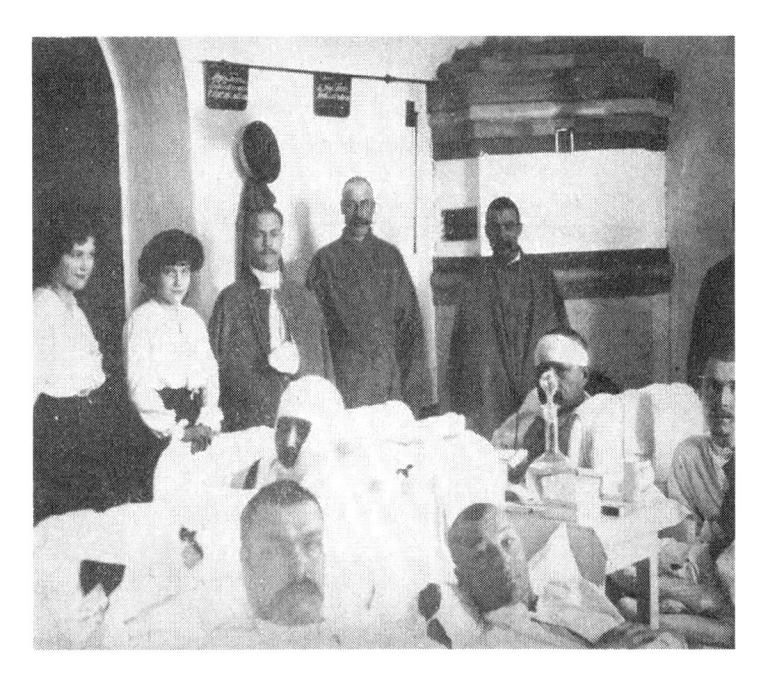

"We went to our infirmary 3 times..." Maria and Anastasia at their infirmary.

Letter from Maria to Nicholas II

17 June, 1916. My dear Papa! Right now I am sitting on the balcony with Mama and Anya. We just finished breakfast. The rain storm is everywhere, and the thunder is very loud. I don't know what we will do. These days Anastasia and I go to our new infirmary very often. It is awfully cozy. I hope that when you return you will come visit us [there]. Every evening we go to the sisters' infirmary, and there we play dobchinsky-bobchinsky. You cannot even imagine how Baron Taube bustles about and argues with Rita Khitrovo[160]. They constantly exasperate each other. The lightning keeps flashing, and Anya crosses herself and says "Oy, please no, I don't want the storm". I will end my

---

[160] Margarita Sergeevna Khitrovo – honorary lady in waiting and friend of the imperial family.

letter, as there is nothing more [to say]. I kiss you affectionately, and Aleksei. Please thank Zhylik for the letter. May God keep you. + Your Kazanetz.

Letters from Anastasia to Nicholas II

21 June, 1916. Tsarskoe Selo. My dear Papa Darling! We just returned from riding, it was rather cold and therefore my hand does not write so well. Yesterday we went to the infirmary as we do every evening […]

24 June, 1916. Tsarskoe Selo. My dear Papa Darling. Maria and I just rolled around in the grass in front of the balcony. It was terribly pleasant and now I am the color of raspberries. We are waiting for Mama and the sisters for breakfast. Sashka will have breakfast with us today. Next to me on the table are your and Aleksei's letters, which were just brought to us. I think that Maria wrote you that we have a new officer at our infirmary from the 10th Sharpshooter regiment, he is wounded in the arm, his name is Zhilinsky, I think, he is sweet although we don't know him well yet. Vik. Erast. is fussing about when and how the 1st Hundred will arrive. Yesterday we four started a bonfire and jumped over it. It was wonderful. We cut off old branches with dull knives and with our hands, and then swung in hammocks. Now there are two hammocks, as Marie has one too and they are hanging in a kilivatorny [?] column. Do you remember that yesterday was 3 years since we had the evening picnic in the Skerries[161] and we all danced and Artemov told [us] all kinds of stories. I read my diary and therefore was reminiscing about every little detail from beginning to end. It was so nice then!!! Everything is as always now. I had a cold and a cough, I was so embarrassed because it is not

---
[161] In Finland

supposed to happen in the summer, but it's a bit better now. So at this moment I just sneezed, you tell me "Bless you", I am very grateful to you for this. Well I will end my letter with masses of kisses to you and Aleksei 1000 times. May God be with you. Sleep well. Your loving. Your loyal and faithful little Kaspiyitz.

Maria's diary entries

29 June. Went to Obednya 4 with Mama at the Palace infirmary. Had breakfast 4 with Mama, Isa on the balcony. Before that rode with Shvybzik and Trina. Went to the new infirmary of the Svodny regiment No.36 with A. Went to the new infirmary with A. Sat with Shurik too. Had tea with Shvybz and the same swung in a hammock. Rode with A. and Isa. Had dinner 4 with Mama on the balcony. Went to the sisters' infirmary. Played croquet and Dobchinsky-Bobchinsky.

1 July. Had lessons. Rode with Anastasia and Trina. Breakfast 4 with Mama and Isa on the balcony. In the afternoon went to our infirmary with A. Sat as usual. Went 4 to the farewell molebna. The 4th Hunded rode on vetka and they passed by us, and we bid [our] farewells. Had tea 4 with Mama on the balcony. Rode with A. and Trina. Had dinner 4 with Mama and Zhylik on the balcony. Went to the sisters' infirmary. Played croquet and D.[obchinsky]-B.[obchinsky].

"In the afternoon went to our infirmary with A. Sat as usual."

Letters from Anastasia to Nicholas II

2 July, 1916. Tsarskoe Selo. My dear Papa Darling! Yesterday Zhylik came over and told us a lot about you all. He had dinner with us. Also yesterday at 4 o'cl. we had moleben in front of the Grand Palace for the 4th Hundred. I feel so sorry for all of them. A lot of them we know by face, but unfortunately not their names. The horses are all packed. They themselves too. After molebna they all passed by us and sang, and when we left we drove through the park to our [train] station and waited as we soon heard the zurna, saw the dust and they appeared. Then we came closer and they all passed by us again, but this time not officially at all as there was no one there but them and the officers, and it was very cold. The kitchens and the carts all passed by us, then the officers climbed down from their horses and we said goodbye to them and left. It was so

sad! After they loaded, they went to the Convoy and they saw them off, sang, etc., and at 10 ¼ they departed. Today we will have a cinematograph for the wounded at the manege. I am very happy, as we are all going too and Mama. Today the weather is warm and sunny. I am writing to you between lessons as [there is] not much time to write. Maria and I swing in the hammocks sometimes and she almost always turns me over and I lie right in my own "fizia" [?]. Well I must end. The Batushka can already be seen on the horizon. I kiss you Papa Darling and Aleksashka 1000 times, you loving loyal and faithful little Kaspiyitz.

Maria's diary entries

3 July. Went to Obednya with Mama at the Pal. infirmary. Rode with A. and Trina. Had breakfast 4 with Mama and Anya on the balcony. Went to our infirmary with Anya. Sat as usual. Had tea and dinner 4 with Mama on the balcony. Rode with A. and Shura. Went to the sisters' infirmary and played croquet and D.B.

7 July.[162] Arrived in Mogilev. Papa and Aleksei came [to meet us]. Had breakfast all together. Rode in a motor across Dnepr to the other bank. Had tea in the train. Had dinner at Stavka on the balcony. Sat with Uncle Sergei and Father Shavelsky. Returned to the train and Papa too, and then he returned home and we went to bed.

---

[162] Again they had arrived at Stavka

The girls with Aleksei at Stavka

9 July. Wrote in the morning. Picked flowers in the field. Had breakfast at Stavka in a tent, sat with Uncle Sergei and Father Shavelsky. Rode in a motor ferry upstream on Dnepr. Got off to walk. Went to Vsenoshnaya. Had dinner in the train. Walked near the train, shot from a revolver at Yulia (Isa's maid).

10 July. Went to Obednya. Walked with T., A., and Count Grabbe in the town garden. At breakfast at Stavka in a tent sat with Uncle Sergei and Uncle Petya. Rode in a motor boat downstream on Dnepr. Had tea in a tent. Went to a cinematograph, it was a

drama and a funny [film]. Had dinner in the train. Syroboyarsky[163] and Lubimov were there – Talked with Gramatin.

11 July. Went to molebna. At breakfast at Stavka in a tent [sat with] Uncle Boris[164] and Konzerovsky. Went upstream on Dnepr in a motor, swam 4 with Isa 17 deg.[rees]. Had tea at the 3rd Hundred Convoy camp. All the officers were there. The Cossacks danced, sang, and played various games. Had dinner in the train. Talked with Golushkin.

"Had tea in a tent." Anastasia and Aleksei at Stavka. Photo was probably taken by Maria.

12 July. Went to a monastery, venerated the Mogilev Mother of God [icon]. At breakfast at Stavka sat with Uncle Georgi and Nilov on the balcony. Rode in motors and walked

---

[163] A.V. Syroboyarsky, one of the officers, former patient at the infirmary.

[164] Grand Duke Boris Vladimirovich.

on the highway. Had tea at Stavka. Returned to the train, bid farewell to darling Papa, Aleksei and others and departed. Had dinner 4 with Isa, Anya, Golushkin, Resin and 2 engineers. Anya was reading Chekhov.

13 July. Did not do anything. Had breakfast and dinner 4 with Isa, Anya, Galushkin, Resin, and 2 engineers. Baked in the sun. Olga was reading Chekhov. Walked at the stations Bologoe, Tosno, M. Vishera. Arrived at Tsarskoe. Went to the new infirmary with Shvybz. Sat with Viktor Er. and Tolstov. Had tea 4 with Mama on the balcony. Unpacked.

Letter from Maria to Nicholas II

16 July. My dear Papa! You will tire your eyes while reading my letter to Aleksei, as I wrote to him on red paper. This morning we are thinking of going riding with Shvybz and Trina. Yesterday afternoon we went to our infirmary, and then to Loman's farm, or rather not his but his daughter's, who gave birth to a son, Roman, two weeks ago, who will be christened by Mama on Sunday. The baby of course was sleeping, and we only looked at him, and then they showed us their rooms. They are very small but cozy. We started going to the sisters' infirmary again in the evenings. I am writing to you while waiting for the Batushka, who probably forgot that he has a lesson with me, and is not coming. Shvybz is sitting across from me and drawing something in an album. We almost never ride with Mama during the day, because we are at our infirmary the entire time. It's time to end, I hear the Batushka's voice in the hallway. I kiss you affectionately. May Christ be with you. + Your loving Kazanetz.

Maria's diary entry

17 July. Went to Obednya 4 with Mama at the Pal. infirmary church. Two rode with Trina. Went to Gr.Pal. with A. Had breakfast and tea 4 with Mama on the balcony. Went to the christening of Roman (son of Nadya Sirotina[165]). Then went to the new infirmary with A. and sat with Viktor Er. Played ping pong with A. Had dinner 4 with Mama on the balcony. Went to the sisters' infirmary, sat, played ruble[166].

Letter from Anastasia to Nicholas II

17 July, 1916. Tsarskoe Selo. My good Papa Darling! Maria and I just came back from the Grand Palace infirmary, and now we are sitting and waiting for Mama and the sisters for breakfast. It is raining now and the weather is not for nothing. We went to Obednya today at the Lower church of the Palace infirmary, because Mama wanted to work at the infirmary. Today at 2 o'clock is the christening of Loman's grandson and Mama will be there as she is the godmother, and we four will go for company, to pretend to be a crowd. Today we ran into Father Shavelsky and Ioannchick, they were coming from the station in a motor. Some of my pictures, which I took in Mogilev turned out, and next time when I write I will send them to you, if Gan[167] deigns to print them for me. I am now imagining all your walks along the Dnepr, it was so nice there! When we stood in church today, I was imagining you standing and what is going on. Have you heard anything about the 4th Hundred, where they are and what they are doing. Well I must end. I give you 1000 big kisses and squeeze you, Papa Darling and Aleksei. May God keep you. Your loving loyal and faithful like a dog and more. Kaspiyitz.

---

[165] Loman's daughter

[166] A table game

[167] The photographer

Maria's diary entry

19 July. Went to Obednya downstairs 4 with Mama. Drew with A. Rode with A. and Trina. Had breakfast and dinner 4 with Mama at the new infirmary. Sat with Tolst.[ov] and others. Had tea 4 with Mama and Anya on the balcony. Was lying down and drawing. Went to the sisters' infirmary. Sat with Count Taube and Nikiforov, played ruble.

"Baked in the sun." The Little Pair with their parents.

Letter from Maria to Nicholas II

20 July. My precious Papa, almost forgot to write to you today, I must have contusion. We will go to the dear Grand Palace with Shvybz now. The sisters are going to Petersburg, and after the Gr. Pal. we will go riding with Mama and Anya. An ensign from my regiment, Shtyrev, is a patient at our infirmary, he was wounded in the leg by an

explosive bullet, but he can walk on crutches. He told [us] a lot about the regiment. Today it is awfully cold and damp, but we still had breakfast on the balcony, albeit in our coats. The motor was supposed to be here already, and it just arrived so I will run. I kiss you affectionately and warmly and squeeze you. May God keep you. Your Kazanetz.

Maria's diary entries

24 July. Went to Obednya at the Pal. infirmary with Mama. Rode with A. and Trina. Had breakfast and tea 4 with Mama on the balcony. Went to the new infirmary with A. Said goodbye to Syroboyarsky. Walked with A., T. and Trina. Had dinner 4 with Mama and Anya. Went to the sisters' infirmary. Played ruble.

25 July. Had lessons. Breakfast 4 with Mama on the balcony. Went to the Gr. Pal. Then to the new infirmary with Shvybz, sat with Vikt. Er. And Tolst. Had tea 4 with Mama and Anya. Packed. Had dinner 4 with Mama. Went 4 to the sisters' infirmary, sat with Pavlov, Bogdanov and Kasianov, played ruble. Before that went to Anya's, saw Alya[168] and Grigori.

Letter from Maria to Nicholas II

25 July. My dear Papa, I am so terribly happy to visit you and Aleksei, after all you are so missed here. I have not packed yet, although not taking a lot of things with me, only the most necessary. I got a letter from N.D., will bring it with me and show it to you, [it] may be interesting for you. Yesterday we finally had a nice day, although not very hot but very pleasant, so a lot of the wounded were lying outside. They brought three

---

[168] Vyrubova's sister

officers to us, 2 Keksumentzy and then a Petrogradetz or a Moscovite. We saw them only for a few minutes as they just brought them in, and the doctor and Lazarev were with them. We had a very successful concert here at our infirmary on 22 July. Please thank P.V.P.[169] for the letters. I will not have the chance to write to him. I kiss you and darling Aleksei affectionately.

Maria's diary entries

26 July. Went to the new infirmary with A. – to say goodbye. Went on the train to Stavka. Had breakfast and tea and dinner 4 with Nastenka, Count Grabbe, Resin, Botkin, Shkuratov and 2 engineers. Walked at the stations Tosno, Bologoe, and M. Vishera. Played with Count Grabbe and Nastenka, read fortunes.

28 July. Were lying down in the field. Ate breakfast in the tent, sat with Uncle Georgi and Gen.[eral] Alekseyev. Sailed on Dnepr on Desna[170]. Had tea in the train. Played various games with the village children. Had dinner 4 with Mama and Papa. Walked.

---

[169] Pyotr Vasievich Petrov, Aleksei's tutor in Russian

[170] Ship

Olga and Anastasia: "Played various games with the village children". Most likely Maria took this photo.

30 July. Went to Obednya. At breakfast sat with Uncle Kyrill, Uncle Georgi. Stayed on the train with Mama. Worked. Had tea all together. Wrote. Had dinner 4 while Mama [ate] with Papa. Walked.

31 July. Went to Obednya. At breakfast sat with Uncle Sergei and Gen.[eral] Alekseyev. Everyone rode in a motor boat up the Dnepr, ran around in the bushes. Had tea at Papa's. Went to a cinematograph "The Chase After Gold" (drama), "The Heroic Act of

Knight Dupron", Sha-no-u, a love novella with a fight (comedy), Tupyshkin's Whip too. Had dinner 4 while Mama with Papa. Mordvinov was here and we were scaring him.

Maria and Anastasia with Mordvinov: "Mordvinov was here and we were scaring him".

3 August. Sat with the children and baked in the sun. Stopped into the church and venerated the Mogilev Mother of God. At breakfast sat with Nilov and Father Shavelsky. Rode in the motor boat up the Dnepr. Walked, lounged in the sun and [ran] around the bushes. Had tea in the train. Said goodbye to Papa and Aleksei. Everyone boarded the

train and left for T.S. Had dinner with Nastenka, Resin [...], Resin's brother, the engineers and Zhylik. Walked at the station. Had tea.

Olga and Anastasia: "Sat with the children and baked in the sun." Maria probably took this photo.

6 August. Went to Obednya 4 with Mama. Rode with A. and Isa. Had breakfast and dinner on the balcony. Went 4 to the G.P. then to the infirmary with A. Had tea 4 with Mama and Anya on the balcony. Went to Vsenoshnaya 4 with Mama. Went 4 to the sisters' infirmary. Played ruble. Before the infirmary stopped at Anya's and saw Grigori and Alya.

7 August. Went to Obednya at the Pal. infirmary with Mama. Rode with A and Trina. Had breakfast and dinner 4 with Mama on the balcony. Went 4 to the sisters' infirmary. Played ruble.

Letter from Maria to Nicholas II

7 August, 1916. My dear darling Papa! Every time we return from Mogilev it seems more difficult and wanting so much more to return to Mogilev. Today we went to Obednya at the Palace infirmary then the sisters and Mama stayed for the dressings while Shvybz and I went riding with Trina. [We] saw the train which arrived from Mogilev with the courier and envied him. Trina and Isa were sick the entire time and only recently got out of bed. We continue going to our infirmary. Because the Tsarskoe [Selo] one does not have enough beds for the officers they will be enlarging our infirmary, the soldiers will be transferred to the old infirmary while the officers will be admitted to the new one in place of the soldiers. It will be a huge infirmary, instead of 12 officers there will be more than 36, and it will be scarier to visit them, such masses [of people]. Our wounded [patients] play tennis now, I don't understand how one of them – [plays] with his left hand, another was wounded in his neck and cannot turn it, but they still love it and play all day long, even those who never knew how to play before, they also play it, and ask us [to play] all the time, but we don't really have time. I kiss you darling and Aleksei affectionately, as warmly as I love you. May Christ be with you + Your Kazanetz. Regards to Vasya and his wife. Also to P.V.P.

Maria's diary entry

8 August. Went to Obednya. Mama received communion. Had lessons. Walked with A. and Trina. Had breakfast 4 with Mama on the balcony. Went to the new infirmary with A. Had tea 4 with Mama and Anya on the balcony. Olga read to me. Had dinner 4 with Mama. Went 4 to the sisters' infirmary. Played ruble.

Letters from Anastasia to Nicholas II

8 August, 1916. Tsarskoe Selo. My Dear Papa Darling! I am now all wet from sweat, as we just took a walk. Today it is very hot. It is awfully pleasant. We are still not used to being here again. It was so awfully nice in Mogilev and living in the train, etc. It is terribly nice to reminisce about how we tormented Mordvinov. I hear [that] Mama and the sisters [just] returned from the infirmary, I will go to breakfast with them, and then finish writing. We finished breakfast and now I am writing to you, and later we will go to our infirmary with Maria. They brought 3 new officers to our infirmary, one of them from the Pavlovsk regiment, one other an artilleryman. We got a letter from Pyotr Vasilievich[171], in which he wrote that you go swimming. How I want to go swimming! Today we went to an early Obednya as Mama received communion, while we pretended to be the public because no one except us and Anya was there, - my "husband" was there but he left. We are studying again and all the same [things] started again. I don't think Mama will go riding as she is too hot and wants to rest. Have you heard anything about the 4th Hundred? Because no one here knows anything and do not get letters. Well I must end. I want to see you and Aleksei again terribly. I send you an awfully big kiss 1000 times,

---

[171] Petrov

may Christ be with you. Your loving loyal and faithful 15 year old Kaspiyitz. Everyone sends kisses.

12 August, 1916. [...] Now when we go to our infirmary, the officers always ask us to play ping pong with them and we play. Some of them play with their left hand rather well, but they can't serve so we have to serve for them all the time, but it is really fun and pleasant to play again. A lot of them sit nearby and watch us play. [...]

Maria's diary entries

14 August. Went to Obednya with Mama. Walked with A. and Trina. Had breakfast and dinner 4 with Mama. Went to the new infirmary with A. Had tea 4 with Mama, Irina and Felix[172]. Went 4 to Vsenoshnaya. Later [went] to the sisters' infirmary, played ruble.

15 August. Went to Obednya 4 with Mama. Rode with A. and Trina. Had breakfast 4 and dinner 4 with Mama. In the afternoon went to the new infirmary with A., saw Shura Pototzky. Had tea 4 with Mama and Aunt Michen. Olga read to me. Went to the sisters' infirmary. Played ruble. Rolled bandages.

Letter from Maria to Nicholas II

15 August. My dear kind Papa! Well it is the fourth day already that we have not played tennis due to awful cold and daily rain. This morning we went to Obednya at the Grotto church and then I rode with Trina and Shvybz. When we passed by the train station I ran into Voeikov and Nilov in a motor. A train from Mogilev will arrive at Tsarskoe at

---

[172] Irina and Felix Yusupovs: the Tsar's niece and her husband, who was later involved in Rasputin's murder.

11.30. It must be so pleasant to have Nik.Pav. with you – The door and windows in our room are open and I am freezing, slowly but surely. Now I need to go to breakfast, but Mama will probably be late. When you are not here they return terribly late. The other day they returned at 13.40. Well I kiss you and Aleksei affectionately. I apologize for this boring letter, but I know of nothing interesting. May God keep you. + Your Kazanetz. Regards to Kolya and Toto[173].

Letter from Anastasia to Nicholas II

16 August, 1916. My precious Papa darling! Thank you for the kisses in the letters. Today we got up rather late because [there were] no lessons. I already drove Mama and the sisters to the infirmary. The weather is really rotten and it is raining now and rather cold, only 10 degrees, and now this [kind of] weather is every day. Yesterday Aunt Michen had tea with us, she returned recently and now lives in Tsarskoe. Yesterday morning we were riding and saw when the train from Mogilev arrived and saw Nilov and Voiekov – who came in a motor, it was very nice to see them. This afternoon all of us and Mama will go to the Grand Palace as we will take [photographs] – this is not so pleasant but that's the way it is. And in the morning Maria and I will go to our infirmary. [...]

Letter from Maria to Nicholas II

20 August, 1916. My dear Papa Darling. It is so nice that we will see you here soon! Today we did not pack much as of course we are taking a lot of things. We just had

---

[173] Count Carl zu Toerring-Jettenbach, known as "Toto" (?)

breakfast with Madame Zizi and also Shura. I apologize that I am writing so badly, but this erasable paper makes such stains. The weather is just awful, rains all the time, we have not seen real sun since Mogilev, everyone is so tired of this. It is really nice to see Mordvinov and Nikolai Pavlovich. I am writing very fast because we must now go to the Grand Palace in order to say goodbye to them, as tomorrow after Obednya we will go to our infirmary before we leave. Tatiana got your letter and went to perform your command. Well that's all the news.

Maria's diary entries

21 August. Went to Obednya with Mama. Then bid farewells at our infirmary with Shvybz. Boarded the train and went to Smolensk. Had breakfast, tea and dinner 4 with Mama, Isa, Resin, Lavrov, Zhylik and 2 engineers. Zhylik read "Anand ee monde s'enuie" to us.

22 August. Arrived in Smolensk, went to the Cathedral and 4 infirmaries. Had breakfast with same as yesterday. Arrived in Mogilev. Everyone met us. Papa had tea with us on the train. Walked around the train. Had dinner 4 with Papa and Mama and Kiki. After dinner we sat in our [train car].

23 August. Went to Molebna. Then had breakfast at Hotel "Bristol" with the staff officers. I sat with Uncle Boris and Count Benkendorf. In the afternoon we went up the Dnepr. Ran around in the bushes. Had tea at Papa's. Went to a cinematograph, they showed the drama "Mystery of Nogorok" and others. Had dinner 4, while Mama [ate] with Papa and Igor. Mordvinov was here and we tormented him. Before dinner talked to Lavrov.

24 August. In the morning [we] wrote and sat in the field with the children. At breakfast in the tent [I] sat with Uncle Georgi and Uncle Kyrill. Went to the left bank in a ferry. 2nd half-Hundred and 3rd half-Hundred came there, officers Papasha, Ponkratov, Gramatin, Shkuropotsky, Kolesnikov and Ergushov. The Cossacks played various games, danced and sang, it was really nice. Then [we] crossed to the right side and ran around in the bushes there. On the way back [we] caught up with the Hundred that was walking along the bank and they rode along us while "djigiting"[174]. Had tea at Papa's on the train. Had dinner 4, while Papa [ate] with Mama. Tormented and scared Toto, played hide and seek.

Anastasia "...sat in the field with the children".

---

[174] Performing various acrobatics on a galloping horse.

28 August. Went to Obednya. At breakfast sat with Uncle Georgi and Dmitri. Went up the Dnepr in a ferry. Later, Papa and I rowed, while Count Grabbe was behind wheel. Had tea at Papa's. Talked with Gramatin. Had dinner 4 with Mama, Papa, Kiki and Anya. Dmitri was here.

30 August. Went to Obednya. At breakfast sat with Uncle Georgi and Dmitri. Went to the same place in motorboats. Children from the city garden were playing there. Returned during a rain storm. Had tea at Papa's. Went to [see] a cinematograph, the continuation of "Mystery of Nogork" and others. Had dinner 4 with Papa and Mama, Dmitri, Anya and Kiki.

4 September. Went to Obednya. Wrote to Zhylik. Papa was at the Headquarters. At breakfast sat with Dmitri and Uncle Sergei. Rode to the upper bridge in motors and walked. Had tea in the train. Said goodbye to Papa, Aleksei, and the children whom we [playfully] pushed into a pit in the ground and left. Had dinner 4 with Isa, Kiki, Khodarsky, Ergushev, P.V.P. and the engineer. P.V.P. read to us.

6 September. Went to "Znamenie". Rode with O. and Trina. Had breakfast with Mama and Isa. Went to our infirmary with A. Had tea with Mama and Uncle Pavel. Had a music lesson. Had dinner 4 with Mama and Anya. Went to the sisters' infirmary. Played ruble.

Letter from Maria to Aleksei at Stavka

Tsarskoe Selo. 6 Sept., 1916. My darling little soul, Aleksei! You cannot even imagine how boring it is to be back at Tsarskoe. Today, when I first woke up I was really surprised to be back in my room. I saw you in my dream, as if we never left you. The head of the infirmary, Baron Kaulbars, also wanted to be in the photo and sat on the little table which you [would normally] put near the bed, Of course the table couldn't hold him, one leg broke, and he fell, it was all very funny. I kiss you and dear Papa affectionately. Your sister, Maria. May God keep you.

Maria's diary entries

7 September. Had Russian language, history and arithmetic lessons. Went to Zolotarev's funeral service, his body was brought over and buried at the brethren cemetery. Had breakfast 4 with Mama, Silaev and Ravpotulo. Went to the G. P. with T. and A. Rode 4 with Trina. Had tea 4 with Mama and Anya. Had dinner, went to Vsenoshnaya and to Anya's with Mama. Grigori and Alya were at Anya's.

8 September. Went to Obednya 4 with Mama. Then played kosti with Shvybz at the new infirmary. Had breakfast 4 with Mama, and dinner. Rode with Mama, Anya and A. Had tea; with Mama, Anya and Kiki. Sat with Isa. Went 4 to the sisters' infirmary and played ruble.

Letters from Maria to Nicholas II

8 September. My sweet and dear Papa, this morning we went to the early Obednya and then to our infirmary with Shvybz, the 4th Hundred Cossacks are such darlings and they talk so much that it makes it hard to leave. They tell [us] all about how it was and how

they were driven around cities, when they were wounded. Such foolish people, they do not know that [they are] the Convoy, and referred to them as Cherkestzy and said that they are not Russian. They were terribly offended. – It was so sad yesterday at the funeral of poor Zolotarev. Now I will go riding with Mama, Shvybz and Anya, while Olga and Tatiana [will go] with Irina. Shegolev came to our infirmary, he has terrible dropsy and we drained one and half buckets of fluid from him. He lost a lot of weight and got old, we saw him today. – And what is Dmitri up to? Time to end. I kiss you and Aleksei affectionately and warmly, like I love you. May God keep you. + Your Kazanetz.

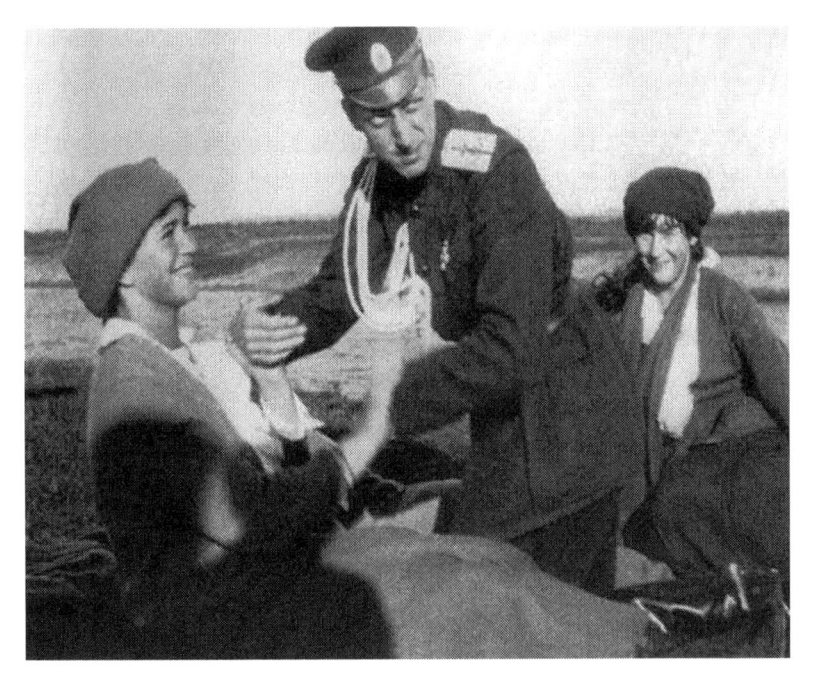

"And what is Dmitri up to?" Grand Duke Dmitri Pavlovich with Maria and Anastasia

12 September. My dear darling Papa! I am sending you the pictures you wanted, and to Svetlichny too. One of the wounded sergeants from the 4th Hundred has recovered

already, but the committee will not allow him to return to the Hundred, but is sending him home to the Caucuses. He is rather unhappy and at first did not even want to agree but they later convinced him. We have not yet played tennis. It's either there is no time, or the weather is bad, raining. Right now I am sitting in the classroom and I am supposed to have a lesson with P.V.P., but he is busy writing the lesson schedule for the winter and is snorting through his nose terribly. He is continuing to write, and I am too. We are now making all sorts of warm clothes for the children who live in Mogilev across from our train. Every time we get back from Mogilev it feels more and more lonesome. You cannot even imagine how I envy P.V.P. who is going to [see] you. But I think he would not allow me [to go instead of him] because as soon as he got to Tsarskoe he caught a dreadful cold. No lesson materialized, P.V.P. only said to [go on] without him. Now there will also be a history lesson, and then I am free and will go riding with Shvybz and Trina. I kiss you and Aleksei affectionately and warmly. May God keep you! Your Kazanetz. Yesterday my new commander came to see me for the first time, he told [me] a lot of nice things about the regiment, so I was very happy even.

Letter from Anastasia to Nicholas II

13 September, 1916. [...] We continue to go to infirmaries and take walks. The other day I rode my bicycle around our park. There were masses of leaves on all paths, and not very cozy!

Maria's diary entries

14 September. Went 4 to Obednya. Then went to the new infirmary with Shvybz, had moleben there. Had breakfast 4 with Mama and Anya. In the afternoon went to the G.P. with T. and A. Rode 4 with Mama, Anya. Had tea with same. Rode with A. and Shura. Had dinner 4 with Mama. The same went to Anya's and saw Alya and Grigori. Went 4 to the sisters' infirmary. Played ruble.

15 September. Had German and French lessons with M. Conrad. The Japanese prince KanYin[175] had breakfast with us. I sat with Uncle Georgi and Uncle Pavel. Rode 4 with Isa. Had tea 4 with Mama. There was music. Read. Had dinner 4 with Mama and Kiki. Went to the sisters' infirmary, played tennis.

Letter from Maria to Nicholas II

16 September. My precious Papa! It is raining hard. In the morning we 4 went to the Vetka with Isa, where Olga's medical train arrived. There were lots of wounded and the guards too. Wonderful people from the Preobrazhensky regiment, so huge. At 12 o'clock 20 minutes we will go to the Feodorovsky Cathedral, where they will have a panikhida for Batushka's son who was killed. I was thinking of going horseback riding this morning, but the weather is rotten, it is raining and damp. All the leaves are rather yellow here and a lot of them fell. Please thank Derevenko very much for the pictures. It was very nice to see Zinovy Ivanovich Isizaki at breakfast yesterday. He showed Olga a menu from afar, reminiscing about how he wrote to her in Mogilev in Japanese. I sat with Uncle Georgi and Uncle Pavel, so it was nice and not embarrassing. Right now I must change into black for the panikhida. These days there are always panikhidas for

---

[175] The cousin of Japanese emperor who visited Russia November-December, 1916.

someone. Today Nastenka will come to see Mama. We have not seen her since the panikhida. Well, farewell, goodbye. May God keep you +. I hug you tightly and kiss you warmly, and Aleksei too. Your Kazanetz. So tiresome that Igor left on a holiday, just when we are not there.

"At 12 o'clock 20 minutes we will go to the Feodorovsky Cathedral.." Colonel Dmitri Loman and his son in front of Feodorovsky Cathedral.

Letter from Anastasia to Nicholas II

17 September, 1916. My good Papa Darling! This morning we had a light but nasty snow, and now it's sunny but cold. [...] We are [the same] as usual. The other day we

played tennis with our wounded officers, they play rather well now as they practice every day.

Maria's diary entries

17 September. Had German, French, Madame Conrad and arithmetic lessons. Had breakfast 4 with Mama and Isa. Went to the new infirmary with A. Then 4 went to the Kazansky cemetery, and the Brethren [one] for Zolotarev. Had tea and dinner 4 with Mama. Went to Vsenoshnaya and 4 to the infirmary. Played ruble. – Drank hot chocolate at our infirmary in the afternoon as it was the birthdays of nurses Maltzev and Adamov.

18 September. Went 4 to Obednya. Then went to the new infirmary and G.P. with A. Had breakfast 4 with Mama. Rode 4 in a motor around Bablovo and Pavlovsk. Had tea 4 with Mama and Anya. Olga read to me and Shvybz. Had dinner 4 with Mama and Kiki. Went to the sisters' infirmary. Played ruble. It was snowing.

21 September. Had lessons, History, Batushka. Rode with A. and Trina. Had breakfast with Mama and A. In the afternoon went to the infirmary with A. and played "Bicks" with Tolstov. Had tea 4 with Mama and Anya. There was music. Had dinner 4 with Mama, and the same went to Anya's, where Grigori, his wife and a monk were. From there 4 went to the sisters' infirmary. Played ruble.

Letters from Anastasia to Nicholas II

21 September, 1916. Tsarskoe Selo. My dear Papa Darling, we just dropped Olga and Tatiana off at their infirmary, and now I am sitting here and waiting for the teacher. Today Olga and Tatiana are going to Petrograd as Tatiana has a committe while we are staying with Mama. I think we will go to my and Maria's infirmary. The Cossacks are still here, one of them left already and these are also getting ready to leave as their wounds are almost healed. Yesterday evening at 6 o'clock I was thinking of you and imagined that you were at a cinematograph. We are now very busy as we have a lot of lessons and most importantly we have to do homework, and today it was cold and there was thin ice on the pond and everything was covered in frost, but it's getting a little warmer now, but the gale is blowing rather strongly. I was just organizing the pictures and have not pasted the Sevastopol ones, as recently Kira[176] gave me the pictures he took there. And now I have to paste them all. I am really sorry that I jump from one thing to another, but this happens unintentionally. Maria just came over and is sending you a big kiss. And I kiss you and Aleksei 1000 times. Your loving loyal and faithful little 15 year old Kaspiyitz.

25 September, 1916. Tsarskoe Selo. My dear Papa Darling. We just finished breakfast and now thinking up of things to do today. The weather is not very nice, cold and damp, everything is wet from rain. Last evening we went to Vsenoshnaya at our Cathedral and Maria Pavlovna was there too, she asked us to take her and she liked it terribly. I think she was only there once before, and only for Obednya at that. Today we went to an early Obednya and then Maria and I went to our infirmary. Viktor Erastovich arrived from Essentuki and Alexander Konstantinovich Shvedov. The former lost some weight, he

---

[176] Kyrill Naryshkin

tells us that his arm is completely well and that he is healthy, not sure how true this is. Please tell Zhylik that I thank him for the letter. So interesting what's going on in "The Mysterious Hand". Zhylik wrote to us but won't be here this Tuesday, I feel sorry for you! I hope my pictures will be ready soon, then I will send them to you. I want to see you so much, Papa Darling. Well time for me to end. I send a terribly big kiss to you and Aleksei. May God be with you. Your loving loyal and faithful Kaspiyetz [sic]. Regards to Nikolai Pavlovich, count Grabbe and your others.

Maria's diary entry

25 September. Went to Obednya. Then to the new infirmary with Shvybz. Vikt. Er. returned from Essentuki[177]. Had breakfast and dinner 4 with Mama. Walked 4 then rode with Trina. Had tea 4 with Mama and Anya. Read. Rode bicycles around the rooms with A. Went 4 to the sisters' infirmary, played ruble.

---

[177] A city in the Caucasus

"Went 4 to the sisters' infirmary..." Maria and Anastasia with Olga and Tatiana in their nurse uniforms at their infirmary.

Letter from Anastasia to Nicholas II

29 September, 1916. Tsarskoe Selo. My precious Papa Darling! Again I am writing to you between lessons. Yesterday we did nothing interesting. Went to our infirmary. In the evening they told us on the telephone that one of the officers has the mumps and there will be 3 weeks of quarantine. We did not see him as he was already in bed when we were there, but at the time they did not know what's wrong with him. How tiresome! Great, just before our departure! – Now we cannot see them at the infirmary. In the evenings Olga and I, and sometimes Maria, fly around our rooms on bicycles, full speed ahead. Olga chases me or I her, very pleasant. Sometimes we fall, but are still alive for now! The lessons just ended and I am going frishtyk-ing with Mama and the sisters, although not sure if they returned yet. In the afternoon we will go to the Grand Palace,

and then I don't know what we will do. The weather is rotten with strong Gale and occasional rain. – Well my Papa Darling it's time to end. I am awfully happy that I will see you [soon]. I kiss you and Aleksei 1000 times. Your loving loyal and faithful Kaspiyitz. Regards to Nik. Pavlovich and others. Everyone sends a big kiss.

Maria's diary entries

30 September. Read and wrote. Had breakfast and dinner 4 with Mama on the couch. Walked 4 and passed by the old infirmary, but did not go in, as Soloviev has something along the lines of mumps. Had tea 4 with Mama and Anya. Went to Vsenoshnaya. 4 with Mama stopped by Anya's where Grigori and the bishops Isidor and Melkhisedek were. Went 4 to the sisters' infirmary, put together a puzzle with Volodya. Played ruble.

4 October[178]. Went to the First and Second Hundred parade, the infantry row. Ergushev, Lavrov, Gramarik and Ganushkin were transferred to the Convoy. At breakfast sat with Uncle Georgi and Maksimovich[179]. At this time the Cossacks sang and then danced very well. Drove to the woods with Papa and the suite, where we walked. Had tea on the train. Then reviewed Grandmama's medical train. [I] went to Aleksei's and played with him. Had dinner 4 with Papa, Mama and Dmitri. Papa read Teffi's[180] stories to us. Had tea.

9 October. Went to Obednya. Ate a sample of the 1st Hundred's [food]. At breakfast sat with Ozerov and Maksimovich. Rode on the Bykov Highway, stopped near the chapel.

---

[178] They are back at Stavka

[179] Konstantin Maksimovich- Commander of the Imperial Apartments

[180] Nadezhda Lokhvitskaya (Teffi) – poet and satirist favored by the Tsar.

Took a walk, saw two trains, [while] the others boiled and fried potatoes. Had tea at Papa's. An Italian military agent came to the Marsengo train. [I] played the guitar and sang. Dinner 4 with Mama, Papa, Isa, Kiki and Anya. Played hide-and-seek, still [with] Mordvinov and Galushkin.

13 October. Wrote. Walked at Likhoslavl st.[ation]. Had breakfast with same as yesterday, and the same with dinner. Vikt. Er. came over, sat with us and smoked and drew. Everyone had tea. After the Tosno station, Vikt. Er. came over again and drew me, and of course I [drew] him, but mine came out badly. After dinner [we] arrived at Tsarskoe Selo. Went to the new and old infirmaries with A. Had tea 4 with Mama. Unpacked.

15 October. Had lessons, German, French, and arithmetic. Had breakfast 4 with Mama and Trina. Went 4 to the G.P., then rode in a motor. Went to the new and old infirmaries with A. Had tea 4 with Mama and Anya. Went 4 with Mama to Vsenoshnaya. Had dinner and went to Anya's, saw Grigori, Mitya[181], Bishop Isador. Went 4 to the sisters' infirmary. Played ruble. Sat with Syroboyarsky, Rita, Volodya, etc.

Letter from Anastasia to Nicholas II

17 October, 1916. Tsarskoe Selo. My precious Papa Darling! Just now I had the arithmetic lesson and now I am free and have to write a lot and do homework. It's so nice that you are coming here! We are all awfully happy. There is snow on the ground today and it's kind of strange, but it is sunny, but 3 degrees below, the weather is so-so.

---

[181] Rasputin's son Dmitri

Yesterday I got a very sweet letter from Mordvinov. Do you know if he sneezed when he got my letter from Orsha. It is so pleasant to remember how nice and fun the time in Mogilev was, and how we used to play hide-and-seek in the evenings. When we were returning it was very nice that Viktor Erastovich was there, otherwise it would have been terribly boring, and he sat with us for a little while in the afternoon and after dinner. It was cozy! Now we have lessons, we go to the infirmaries and all is the same there. We do not have any new wounded at our infirmary, only an officer from Maria's regiment, a Kazanetz. Mama is going to her infirmary for dressing changes in the mornings for now. Yesterday afternoon we rode with Mama, Anya and all four of us. Did not run into too many people, almost no one was out walking. Yesterday Mama received Countess Karlova and her daughter Merica, as she is planning to get married in November, so she returned, [she is] rather cute. Maria just walked by here and sends you a big kiss. I think she now has a history lesson. Well, my Papa Darling it's time for me to end. I send you and Aleksei an awfully big kiss 1000 times. Regards to Mordvinov. May God keep you. Your loving loyal and faithful little 15 year old Kaspiyitz.

Maria's diary entries

20 October. Went to Petrograd with Papa, Mama, O. and T. to the Fortress[182], for the funeral Obednya for Grandpapa[183]. Had breakfast 5 with Papa, Mama and Igor. Walked 4 with Papa and Mama [rode] in an equipage. Had tea and went to Vsenoshnaya, the same confessed. Had dinner 4 with Papa, Mama and Igor.

---

[182] St Peter and Paul Fortress in St Petersburg.

[183] Anniversary of death of Alexander III

21 October. Everyone received communion. Then had tea. Walked with Papa and A. Had breakfast 5 with Mama, Papa and Ioann. Went to the new and old infirmaries with A. Played billiards with A., Medvedev and Lozhnov. Had tea 4 with Mama and Papa. The 2 Makarovs, 2 Derevenko 1 Derevenko and Tanya Raftopuldo [sic] came over for Aleksei's cinematograph. Went to Vsenoshnaya with Mama. Had dinner 4 with Papa and Mama and Ioann. Went to Anya's with Mama and Papa, and Grigori was there. Sat and drank tea.

Letter from Maria to Nicholas II

30 October. My dear Papa darling! Today is already two years that the dear Grand Palace infirmary exists, and therefore we must go to a concert there. Your friend Lersky will be there, I am happy to see him as he usually tells such nice funny stories. I am now sitting at Mama's. In the morning we went to an early Obednya and after that to our infirmary. At first we went to [see] the lower ranks then the officers. There we played billiards. I played like swine of course, because it is hard without practice. Yesterday Viktor Erastovich came to our infirmary. He wins over everyone in billiards. Time to end as I have to complete [sewing] two shirts for the officers who are leaving our infirmary and are bidding their farewells to Mama at 6 o'clock. I kiss and squeeze you darlings affectionately. May God keep you. + both . Your Kazanetz.

Letters from Anastasia to Nicholas II

31 October, 1916. Tsarskoe Selo. My dear Papa Darling! Well it is again my turn to write to you. Now I will have my last lesson with Pyotr Vasilievich as he is leaving today. I am very envious of him, he will see you tomorrow already! Forgive me that I'm

writing so violently, but this quill scratches terribly and nothing comes out. Right now it is raining and rather nasty as it is windy and a bit cold - Tatiana Andreyevna Gromova wrote and described to us how you and Aleksei came to their infirmary at Aunt Olga's. It was written in a very funny way and very detailed, even what you said, she was awfully happy to see you. Yesterday we went to a concert at the Grand Palace. They were celebrating a two year anniversary of their infirmary. It was rather nice. Your friend Lersky was there and Mama saw him for the first time and she liked it. They sang and talked a lot etc., but generally everything is the same. We continue playing billiards a bit at our infirmary, sometimes it turns out well - and then I'm happy. Viktor Erastovich comes over and plays sometimes and of course better than anyone else.... Right now Olga's cat is running around here, I think she grew and is rather cute. I think Igor is coming to [see] you too with this letter, you are probably very happy about this! ... Well now, my dear Papa! I send you and Aleksei a 1000 awfully big kisses, may God be with you. Your loving loyal and faithful Kaspiyetz [sic].

"Right now Olga's cat is running around here, I think she grew and is rather cute." Tatiana reading a book while petting the family cat on the imperial yacht. Olga is in the background. Either Maria or Anastasia probably took this photo.

Maria's diary entry

2 November. Had lessons. History and Batushka. Went to the old infirmary with A. Had breakfast and dinner 4 with Mama. Went to the G.P. with T. and A. then to the new infirmary with A. Played billiards with Loginov and Dmitri. Had tea 4 with Mama and Anya. Talked on the telephone with Aleksei in Mogilev. There was some music. Went to Isa's, Sasha Melikova was there. Went 4 to the sisters' infirmary. Sat with Syroboyarsky, Nikiforov and Ulanov. Then with Mama at Anya's, Grigori and Bishop Isidor were there.

Letters from Anastasia to Nicholas II

5 November, 1916. My precious Papa! We just got up and now having had the morning milk I am alone at a lesson. I don't know where Maria is. Well, everything is as always. The only thing [different] is that I don't have a lesson. I slept well and dreamed of you. It snowed very little, and the trees are covered with frost and it is rather cold. I don't think we did much yesterday, rode and went to our infirmary – played billiards. And in the evening we went to Mama's infirmary – as usual. Ah, it started snowing now! […]

9 November, 1916. […] Yesterday evening we four and Mama rode around, and then went to the infirmaries. Then we had lessons and in the evening, went to the infirmary again. Well, that was our whole day. […]

Letter from Maria to Nicholas II

10 November. Papa my dear! Such joy to be going to [see] you. I was afraid that we would not get to you before winter. Just now I accompanied Mama, Olga and Tatiana to the infirmary. I will have a lesson with Batushka, and then I am thinking of taking a walk or else riding with Shura. In the afternoon we will go to the medical train named after Mama. They will have moleben there and tea with the Metropolit. Of course Loman arranged this. Yesterday we went to our infirmary with Shvybz. Viktor Erastovich was there too, and we played billiards with him and one [other] wounded [patient]. It is terribly nice to see chests in the hallway, gives one the feeling that we are going soon. This time Nastenka is coming with us. I don't think Isa is too happy, but I don't care as I like Nastenka more, she is after all more simple than Isa. Time to end. I will also write to

Aleksei's P.V.P., and I kiss you Papa my darling very very affectionately. May Christ be with you. + Your very own Kazanetz. The pictures which A. is in – [give] to Aleksei, the rest are for you, the ones you wanted.

Maria's diary entries

2 December. Had lessons, English, Russian and Batushka. Had breakfast 5 with Papa, Mama and count Totleben. Walked 4 with Papa, while Mama in an equipage. Went to the new and old infirmaries with A. Played kosti. Had tea with A. upstairs. Went 5 to Anya's infirmary. Sasha Makarov's concert, De Lazari and accordion. There was music. Prepared homework. Had dinner 4 with Papa and Mama. The same [were] at Anya's with Grigori, and had tea. Talked nicely.

4 December. Went to Obednya 5 with Papa and Mama and the same had breakfast with Toto. Showed Toto our rooms. Walked 5 with Papa. Saw off Papa and Aleksei (they went to Mogilev). Went 4 to a concert at the G.P. Had tea 4 with Mama and Anya. Went to the old infirmary with A., played checkers. Stopped by Nastenka's and Isa's. Had dinner 4 with Mama, the same went to the sisters' infirmary. Played checkers with Shareiko.

9 December. Went to the old infirmary with A. Had breakfast and dinner 4 with Mama. Rode with Isa. Went to the new infirmary with A., played kosti and the gramophone. Had tea 4 with Mama and Syroboyarsky, who is going to his reserve platoon. There was

music. Nastenka and Isa stopped by. Went 4 to the sisters' infirmary, then to Anya's with Mama; Grigori and Lili Dehn [were there].

Letter from Anastasia to Nicholas II

10 December, 1916. Tsarskoe Selo. [...] This afternoon we will go to the consecration of Aleksei's infirmary, which is at the Sharpshooter's new barracks. This infirmary moved here from Petrograd, it was at Madame Sukhomlinova's before this. [...] It is snowing here occasionally and the gale is blowing a bit. We are [the same] as usual. Nothing new at our infirmary. Shegolev is not feeling well, he is very weak and nods off sweetly from weakness and he does not look well [...]

Anastasia and Olga looking at a photo album

Maria's diary entries

10 December. Had lessons, German, French and arithmetic. Had breakfast 4 with Mama and Isa. The same went to the consecration of the barracks infirmary of the 3rd Sharpshooter regiment. Went to the Old and New infirmaries with A., Vikt. Er. was at the

latter. Had tea, went to Vsenoshnaya. Had dinner at Anya's with Grigori and at the sisters' infirmary. From the infirmary [went] directly to the train 4 with Mama, where we spent the night, and during the night departed to Novgorod.

11 December. Arrived in Novgorod, there was a Greeting at the station. Went to the Sofiisky Cathedral. There was a bishop's Obednya, then [we] venerated the Relics of various saints. Walked through to the Patriarch's chamber, they have an infirmary downstairs.

12 December. Arrived at Tsarskoe Selo. Went to the old and new infirmaries with A. Had breakfast and tea 4 with Mama. Rode in a troika with Isa. Sat and read. There was music. Had dinner 4 with Mama and Grigori at Anya's. Went to the infirmary 4 with the sisters. Played ruble, then checkers with Shareiko.

Letter from Anastasia to Nicholas II

15 December, 1916. Tsarskoe Selo. My Dear Papa Darling! You already know well about our trip to Novgorod as I think Olga wrote a lot about it. In my opinion it went very well! It was so cozy to sleep in the train and the feeling was a little like we were going to see you in Mogilev. Maria just walked over and sends you a big kiss. Well Christmas is so soon! We are all waiting for you! This Tuesday I was thinking of you and imagining how you were going to the theater. Right this minute I got a letter from Zhylik and the continuation of "The Mysterious Hand". I have not yet read it so we will read it aloud all together, more interesting that way! I think that today Igor is leaving you, on 15 December? We just had breakfast with Kozhevnikov, who arrived in Petrograd a few days ago, but soon he is leaving again. He told us masses of interesting things – how

their transfer went and etc. He remains the same. Well now, Papa my Darling it's time for me to end. May Christ be with you. I send you and little Aleksei an awfully big kiss. Your loving loyal and faithful little 15 year old Kaspiyitz.

Author's Note

By late 1916, things in St Petersburg were not peaceful and getting progressively worse. Riots became a common occurrence because of people's anger about the protracted and mismanaged war, as well as regular food shortages. The political slogans "Down with the war!" and "Down with autocracy!" were seen and heard more and more often. No longer were the attempts to disperse the commonly seen demonstrators successful.

Anger at Grigori Rasputin's involvement with the imperial family escalated as well. Even though this perception was greatly exaggerated, he nevertheless was seen as the puppet master of the imperial couple, appointing government officials at will, which further damaged the Tsar's reputation on all levels. Hence, 1916 ended with the murder of Rasputin, committed by misguided members of the Tsar's extended family, who believed that getting rid of the reviled peasant would help rehabilitate the monarchy. But it was much too late.

Maria's diary entries

17 December. Had lessons, German, M. Cond. and arithmetic. Had breakfast 4 with Mama. Went to the old infirmary with A. Rode in a troika with O., T., Isa. Had tea 4 with

Mama and Anya, the same went to the Vsenoshnaya at home and had dinner. After dinner Lili Dehn came over. Bad news, Grigori disappeared since last night. No one knows where he is.

18 December. Went to Obednya. Mama and Anya received communion. Everyone sat with Lili Dehn. Had breakfast 4 with Mama. Sat together again and had tea. Walked with O., A., Lili and Titi. Went to our infirmary with A. Sat. Had dinner 4 with Mama, Anya, Kiki and Lili. Sat all together. Nothing new is known about Grigori, they suspect Dmitri and Felix[184].

21 December. Went to Grigori's funeral 4 with Papa and Mama and others. He was buried at Anya's construction. Had lessons, history and Batushka. Had breakfast 4 with Papa and Mama. Went to the old infirmary with A. Walked with Papa. Went to the new infirmary with A, and Vikt. Er. was there. Had tea 4 with Papa and Mama near Aleksei, he has worms in his belly. There was music. Went to Anya's, saw Matryona, Varya[185] and Akulina[186]. Had dinner 4 with Papa, Mama and Sandro. Anya was here. Papa read.

22 December. Went to the old and new infirmaries with A. Had breakfast 5 with Papa, Mama and Toto. Sat at Mama's with Anya, Lili and Zina. Had tea 4 with Papa and Mama. Sat at Mama's. Had dinner 4 with Papa, Mama and Toto. Walked with Toto. Anya was here. Sat and worked.

---

[184] On the night of December 16-17, Grigori Rasputin was murdered by several conspirators, including Grand Duke Dmitri Pavlovich and Prince Felix Yusupov.

[185] Matryona and Varya were Rasputin's daughters.

[186] Akulina Laptinskaya- Rasputin's housekeeper. Was also a nurse at the imperial infirmary.

28 December. Went to the old infirmary with A. The Mertopolitan came over to praise Christ. Had breakfast 4 with Papa and Mama, Anya and Groten. Went 4 to the G.P. Walked 4 with Papa. Went to a concert at the new infirmary with T. and A. Plevitskaya was there and Vaganova danced. Had tea 4 with Papa and Mama, dinner with same. Anya was here, pasted in the album with her and Shvybz. – Aleksei was in bed all day, his arm hurts and [he] slept badly.

31 December. Went to the old and new infirmaries with A., played billiards with Kotov and Tolstov. Had breakfast and dinner with Papa, Mama and Nicky. Walked with Papa, O. and T. Went to the nanny school Christmas party with T., A. and Nastenka. Had tea 4 with Papa and Mama. Went to Vsenoshnaya with Papa. Read fortunes with Anya, sharpened wax and peeled the shells[187]. Had tea. Went to moleben 3 with Papa and Mama at the house church.

---

[187] Candle wax and egg shells were used to read fortunes, a tradition on New Year's Eve.

Chapter Four: 1917

Author's Note

The members of the Duma, Russia's legislative body, now began to blatantly criticize the Tsar's government, and finally urged him to abdicate. As far as they were concerned, Nicholas II's credibility and authority was so impaired that he could no longer rule Russia effectively. Abdication was seen as the only solution. After a long and painful reflection, the Emperor decided to renounce the throne for himself as well as for his son, because of Aleksei's terminal illness. He abdicated in favor of his younger brother Grand Duke Michael, who proceeded to give up his claim to the throne shortly after. With a stroke of a pen, the 300 year old rule of the Romanovs was over.

During the early months of 1917, all the imperial children, except Maria caught the measles (Maria fell ill later). During those days Maria became the main support to her mother, Empress Alexandra. She described her experiences in a letter to her father below.

Letter from Maria to Nicholas II

3 March. 1917 Tsarskoe Selo. Our dear and sweet Papa! I am always with you in my thoughts and prayers. The sisters are still lying in a dark room, while Aleksei is already bored with it and therefore lying in the playroom, where they do not shut any windows.

Today we molded bullets from tin with Zhylik and he [Aleksei] loved it. Mama is full of energy, although [her] heart is not completely in order. I spend almost entire days with Mama lately, because I am the only one now who remains healthy and able to walk. I also sleep with her, to be close by in case something needs to be said or someone wants to see her. Lili sleeps here in the red room near the dining room sofa where Olga used to lie. She is terribly sweet and helps us all a lot. From our windows we can see our Cossacks and soldiers. Yesterday I went around the cellar with Mama, and saw how they all settled in there. There is complete darkness in the cellar as we do not have electricity during the day. The soldiers were very sweet and when we passed by them, they jumped up from the straw where they were resting and greeted Mama. A porter was leading us with a candle and commanded the soldiers "on attention". In the evening I saw Vikt. Erastovich, he said that Vershikov, who was under house arrest like the rest of Convoy in Petrograd, walked here on foot from Petrograd during the night. We all kiss you affectionately and warmly, our dear darling Papa. May God keep you. + Your children. Yesterday afternoon we had moleben, they brought Znamenie Mother of God icon from the church to the sisters. We all felt better somehow the entire day after that. – Papa darling, we all heard and believe that the Lord will never abandon the One who did all he could for all of us. We kiss you warmly many times over. God is always with you and our friend in heaven[188] also prays intensely for you, and everyone, everyone – our thoughts of you never leave us even for a minute.

---

[188] She is referring to Rasputin.

Maria with Nicholas in early 1917.

Author's Note

In early March, representatives of the Provisional Government, which was set up after the Tsar's abdication for the interim, arrived at Stavka in Mogilev and arrested the Tsar, taking him back to Tsarskoe Selo. There, the rest of the family was also placed under house arrest at the Alexander Palace.

Many of the imperial retinue members elected to remain with the family after their imprisonment. Despite everything the children's education continued with their tutors. At this time there was hope that the newly deposed Tsar and his family will be able to go abroad to England. But King George V ultimately decided he could not afford to risk his own people's anger and withdrew his offer of asylum to his first cousins. As history would show, this decision produced a fatal outcome for Russia's former imperial family.

Postcard from Anastasia to Lili Dehn. 10 April, 1917.

Thank you so much for the postcard, dear Tili. Maria is also very grateful. I now take walks with Papa, Tatiana and Aleksei when it is warm out, And how are you? I send you good wishes. I kiss you and the little one affectionately. Your loving Anastasia. 10th April, 1917. T.S.

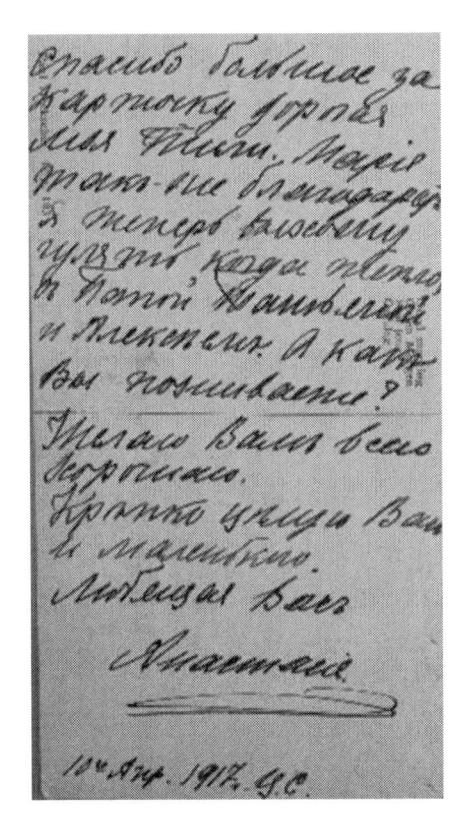

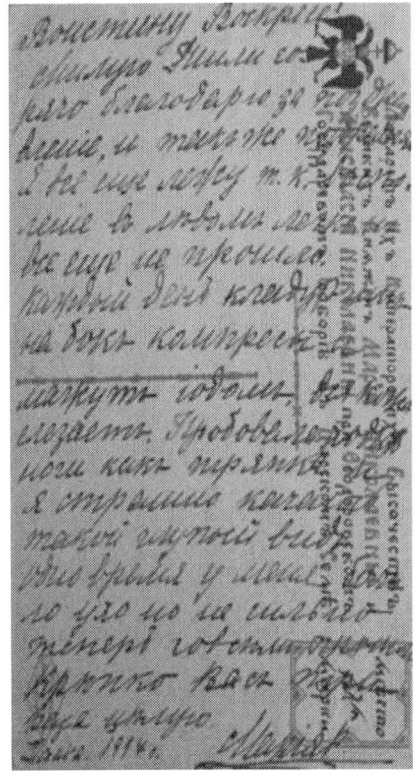

Postcards to Lili Dehn from Anastasia (left) and Maria (right) (Courtesy of Beinecke Library)

Postcards from Maria to Lili Dehn

"Indeed He Has Risen! Darling Tili, I thank you immensely for your [holiday] greetings, and also send you [good] wishes. I am still in bed as [I have] inflammation in [my] left lung, [it] still has not gone away. Every day they put a compress on my side, and spread iodine so my skin is peeling. [I] tried to walk but [my] legs are like rags and I am swaying awfully, looking so foolish. At one point I had ear ache but [it was] not too bad, now we all talk loudly. I kiss you affectionately three times.   Easter. 1917.   Maria"

"I heartily thank my dear Tili for the sweet little card." Postcard from Maria to Lili Dehn (Courtesy of Beinecke Library)

3rd May, 1917. I heartily thank my dear Tili for the sweet little card. I have been wanting to write to you for a long time but somehow was not able. How are you and the little one doing? We all go out in the garden daily. [It is] so pleasant to sit out in the sun. Someone probably already wrote you that we are planting a vegetable garden. It is really fun to dig the soil and cart it around, I already have blisters on my hands. We just had lessons with Olga and Mama. I kiss you and the little one very very affectionately. Your M. Did you have any news from your husband lately?

"We all go out in the garden daily. [It is] so pleasant to sit in the sun."   Maria, Olga, Anastasia and Tatiana resting near the vegetable garden they worked in. "It is really fun to dig the soil..." Tatiana and Anastasia digging in the Alexander Park vegetable garden.

Postcards from Anastasia to Lili Dehn.

T.[sarskoe] S.[elo]. 5th June, 1917. My dear good Tili, thank you so much for the greetings and the English birdy! I would like to kiss and squeeze you in person. Last night they pierced my ears and I put on earrings. I must write a lot more [letters], therefore will end. I mentally kiss the sweet Tili and the little one affectionately. Please write. Your A.

6th June, 1917. My dear Tili! I apologize terribly that I have not written to you for so long, and did not even thank you for the card. So how are you all dear and your little one? I am so happy that D[illeg] is helping him and he will be completely well. I am writing to you from the red room, Olga is sitting by the window and reading, the others are on the [... incomplete...]

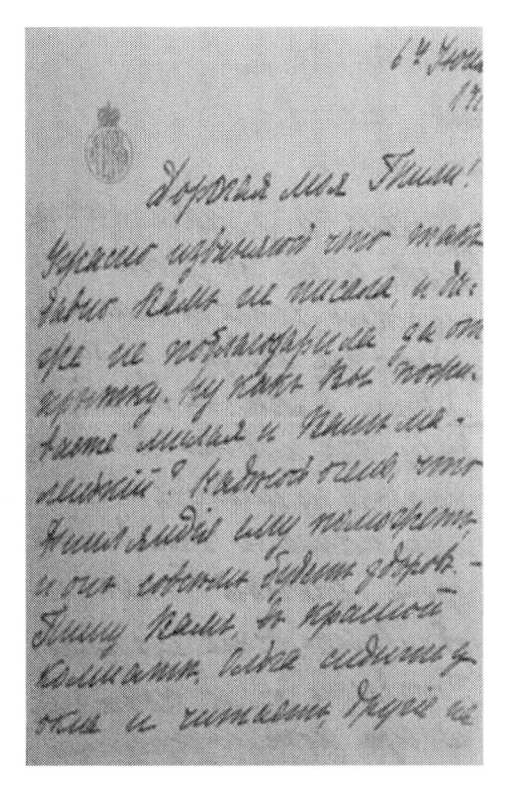

Postcard from Anastasia: "My dear Tili!..." (Beinecke Library)

Author's Note

After several months of house arrest during which there was an investigation to make sure no treason was committed by the German born Alexandra (as rumor had it), the

Provisional Government decided to remove the prisoners from Tsarskoe Selo "for their own greater safety", and send them to a prosperous Siberian town of Tobolsk. At the dawn of the first day of August, 1917, in strictest confidence a train bearing a Japanese Red Cross flag pulled out of the imperial train station heading eastward towards Siberia. Inside were Grand Duchesses Maria and Anastasia and their family, along with a number of their retinue who were willing to share their exile.

Among numerous chests which held family treasures such as books, icons and jewels, the children packed their army cots, which they set up in a corner bedroom of the Governor's house - the family's new prison in Tobolsk. For a few months, life in Tobolsk was relatively comfortable for the imperial captives. The children continued their lessons, and the family still had servants, doctors and cooks at their disposal. They were permitted to go outdoors with supervision, and to attend local church services. They entertained themselves by putting on plays, reading newspapers and books aloud, and taking walks. The attitude of the locals was sympathetic towards the former Tsar and they regularly received gifts of food which supplemented their menu.

The farewellcard handmade by the imperial family for their friends upon their departure to Siberia.
(Beinecke Library)

Postcard from Anastasia to V. G. Kapralova[189]. 10 August, 1917. Tobolsk.

Dearest Vera Georgievna, We arrived here safely. For now we are living on the steamer as the house is not ready. As I write, it is wet with rain. M is lying down as she caught a cold, but she is already better now. Send our regards to [your] sister and Evg. Aleks. I hope you are all well. All the best. We kiss you. Don't forget us. Excuse the smudges.

Letter from Anastasia to a friend[190]. 17 August, 1917. Tobolsk.

---

[189] Vera Georgievna Kapralova: one of the nurses who worked at the "Little Pair's" infirmary

[190] This letter was originally written in English and all Anastasia's mistakes were kept intact.

My dear Friend. I will describe to you who [sic] we travelled. We started in the morning and when we got in to the train I went to sleap [sic], so did all of us. We were very tierd [sic] because we did not sleap [sic] the whole night. The first day was hot and very dusty. At the stations we had to shut out [sic] window curtanse [sic] than [sic] nobody should see us. Once in the evening I was looking out we stopped near a little house, but there was no station so we could look out. A little boy came to my window and asked: "Uncle, please give me, if you have got, a newspaper." I said: "I am not an uncle but and anty [sic] and I have no newspaper." At the first moment I could not understand why did he call me "Uncle" but then I remembered that my hear [sic] is cut and I and the soldiers laught [sic] very much. On the way many funy [sic] things happened, and if I shall have time I shall write to you and our travell [sic] father [sic] on. Good by [sic]. Don't forget me. Many kisses from us all to you my darling. Your A.

Contemporary postcard with the view of the governor's house in Tobolsk.

Letters from Maria to V.G. Kapralova.

To: Vera Georgievna Kapralova, Sister of Mercy at [Feodorovsky] Infirmary in Tsarskoe Selo. Tobolsk. 20th September, 1917.   I thank you very much, my sweet Vera Georgievna, for the card. I was remembering you on the 28th of August in particular. It was so nice at the infirmary. We think of all of you very very often. Do you ever see the former nurses and Olga Vasilievna? Please pass this letter to Katya. All this time we've had wonderful weather and [it is] even hot in the sun. But today it is snowing and strong wind. Right now I am sitting in my room. We live in one room all 4, so it is not lonesome. Our windows look over the street and we often look at the passers-by. Well, and what do you do my dear?

I continue writing on 21st September. The snow is already laying on the ground. And what kind of weather do you have? Is it still warm or cold already? I remember how we used to go to the infirmary last year. – Did you finish embroidering your appetizing blue pillow case with the grapes? Anastasia kisses and thanks you for the card, she will write one of these days. We just took a walk, went to the garden and dug for rutabaga. Here in the garden we only have rutabaga and cabbage. Thank Verochka and Evg. Aleks. very much for remembering [us], we kiss them affectionately. Do you know anything about the health of Anna Pavlovna[191]? Forgive me for so many questions, but I want to know so much what everyone is doing and how they all are. I wish you all the best, my dear, and embrace you warmly. I hope that you got our letter in time for the holiday,

---

[191] Possibly one of the infirmary nurses

Heartfelt greetings to your sister and all the acquiantances. Does Kolibri and others write to you? How did they settle in at the Infirmary No.36? Probably it is very cozy, were you there? Well time to end. M.

Tobolsk. 15th October, 1917. Heartfelt thanks to you, dear Vera Georgievna for the cards, which got here although were addressed wrong, as we live in city center in the house of the former governor. I hope you have completely recovered by now, - So tiresome to be sick in bed. How did you like Roman? He probably grew a lot since last summer. And what is Loshnov up to at O.V.? Did you run into anyone we know from the infirmary? There is not much to write about myself, we are all [the same] as usual. Went to Obednya at 8 o'cl. in the morning today. The church is close to [our] house, you just have to walk across the city gardens and the street. We just had tea and are now sitting all together. Our brother is playing with Kolya[192], who is allowed to come over only on holidays. – Regards from me to your sister and the acquiantances who have not forgotten us. Did Kartasheva write? I wish you good health and all the best, my dear. I embrace you warmly for remembering [us]. May God keep you. M.

Letter from Maria to Ksenia Alexandrovna in Crimea. 21 October, 1917

21 October, 1917. My sweet Aunt Ksenia. How are you, and all the others. I have not written to you from Tobolsk yet, for which I apologize. Although they say that winter starts early here, we do not have it [yet]. The snow is here only in patches, and [it is] not freezing, no less than 5 deg. But it is sunny almost every day. We started our lessons. We study with Zhimer, Mr Gibbs, Trina, [our] parents etc. – And your boys, they are

---

[192] Kolya Derevenko, the physician' son.

probably also studying intensely now. We go outside twice a day. Walk in the yard and the garden, about which the sisters probably wrote you. – Yesterday we had a funerary Vsenoshnaya here at the house, and this morning an obednitza[193]. 4 nuns from the Ioannovsky monastery from outside the city always sing at the services. They say it is very beautiful there in the woods among the mountains. They bring us milk and eggs from the monastery. – How is your nephew Tikhon[194]. What is dear Aunt Andr. up to. Kiss her for me. I hope that she received the letter I sent her back in September, does Grandmama leave the house, or is she still too weak. – The dentist Kastritsky came here and we are all treated by him. We are not doing anything interesting, which is why my letters turn out very boring. [I] really want to know so much more about you, what you are doing. – Did Vasya move in with his brothers, or still living with Nana[195]. I kiss her, it is probably fun for her to go see Tikhon and play with them. I kiss you all affectionately, and especially you, my sweet darling. I think of you very very often. May the Lord keep you.   Your Maria.   If you have any new pictures from the Crimea, of yourself and Aunt Olga, I would be so happy to get them. [I] embrace [you].

Author's Note

In October of 1917, the Bolshevik party headed by Vladimir Lenin overthrew the Provisional Government. As a result, conditions in the faraway Governor's house began to deteriorate. They were no longer allowed to go out of the house except into the

---

[193] Short Obednya

[194] Grand Duchess Olga Alexandrovna's new baby with her second husband Nicholas Kulikovsky.

[195] Elizabeth Franklin, Olga Alexandrovna former governess

courtyard, and their food rations became a lot scarcer. Most of their friends and retinue were no longer allowed to see or speak to them freely.

Letter from Maria to V.G. Kapralova.

14th November, 1917. Tobolsk. I thank my sweet Vera Georgievna warmly for letters No's 3 and 4. It was very nice to find out that you are alive and well. How are you feeling after the illness? I hope you are not too weak. Everyone sends thanks for the greetings, [they] send regards to you, Ak.Iv. […]. Aleksei sends a warm kiss. Klavd.[ia] Mikh.[ailovna][196] teaches [us] Literature and History lessons, I think you know her from school. We have snow on the ground but it is rather warm, even melting these days. Our only acquaintance here is the son of one of the service women, Tolya, who is 6 years old. He reminds us of Vit'ka Vor. We play in the yard with him and inside in [our] rooms, he really amuses us. It is so nice to play with the little ones, as we love children. When we went to Mogilev last year we had a lot of children acquiantances in the village, and we wrote about them often. It so happens that today you celebrated the anniversary of [illeg], does it still exist and where is the staff from there? Did O.V. stay with her husband in Peterhof? Did the Loginovs leave as they planned? I still shudder to think that Verochka got married. We wrote to her in Peterhof after her wedding, I don't know if she got it. I wish you all the best, darling. I kiss you and your sister too. May God keep you.   Maria.

Postcard from Maria to Nikolai Demenkov. 22 November, 1917. Tobolsk.

---

[196] Klavdia Mikhailovna Bitner

Heartfelt congratulations for [your] day of the angel and wishing you all the best in life. So sad that we have not heard from you in so long. How are you? This is our house. The rooms are appetizing and bright. Our windows face this street (Freedom St.). They had set up bars from the booth to the little fence where we take walks. We sit on the balcony especially often. [We] reminisce about the happy times, the games, Ivan. What are you up to? Regards to all who remember us. We are sending warm greetings. May God keep you. M. 22nd November, 1917.

"This is our house. The rooms are appetizing and bright." Front and back of the postcard from Maria to Nikolai Demenkov. Under the photo it is written: "Tobolsk. Freedom Street. N.D.D."

Letter from Anastasia to Anna Vyrubova. December 10, 1917. Tobolsk.

My darling and dear: Tender thanks to you for your little gift. It was so nice to get it, reminding me especially of you. We think and speak of you often, and in our prayers we are always together. The little dog you gave [us] is always with us and is very nice. We have arranged our rooms comfortably and all four live together. We often sit at the windows looking at people passing by, and this gives us distraction [...] We have acted in little plays for amusement. We walk in the garden behind high fence. God bless you.
AN

Letter from Maria to Z.S. Tolstaya[197]. Tobolsk. 10 December, 1917.

[...] We live quietly, take walks twice a day as usual. The weather is nice, but the other day it was very cold. You must still have warm weather? I am so envious that you can look at the wonderful sea! This morning at 8 we went to Obednya. We are always so happy when they let us go to church, of course one cannot compare this church with our Sobor[198], but still better than [having service] in the room. Right now we are all sitting in our room. The sisters are also writing, the dogs are running around and begging to sit on our laps. I remember Tsarskoe Selo so often, and our merry concerts at the infirmary; do you remember how much fun it was when the wounded used to dance; we also remember our walks to Pavlovsk and your small equipage, the morning rides past your house. It all seems so long ago. Doesn't it? Well, it's time for me to end. I wish You

---

[197] Countess Zinaida Sergeyevna Tolstaya, who at the time was living in Odessa on the Black Sea.

[198] Feodorovsky Cathedral in Tsarskoe Selo

all the best and kiss You and Dalya[199] affectionately. Heartfelt regards to all your [family]. Maria

Letter from Maria to Anna Vyrubova.

Tobolsk, Dec. 1917. Hello my dear! I have not written to you in so long, dear, [I] was so happy to get your little note. It is so sad that we do not see each other, but God will grant [it so] that we meet again and then it will be such joy. We live in a house which you had visited[200]. Do you remember the rooms? They are very cozy, especially when one's own things are everywhere. We walk every day, twice. There are nice people here too. I remember you darling, daily and love you so much. M. Gibbs gave us your cards, it was so pleasant to have them. We wear the gift brooches. [We] sniffed all your perfumes, it reminded us so much of you. I wish you all the best from God and kiss you warmly and affectionately. Do not be lonesome, Christ is with you. Your much loving M. Regards to all of yours.

---

[199] Tolstaya's daughter

[200] Vyrubova visited the governor's house when she was in Tobolsk a few years earlier.

Chapter Five: 1918

From Aleksei's letter to his tutor. Tobolsk, 7 January, 1918.

[…] The sisters and I had rubella, and Anastasia was the only healthy one and walked with Papa.[…]

Tatiana pulling Aleksei in a sled in front of the Governor's house.

Postcard from Maria to Anna Vyrubova. 22 January, 1918.

Tobolsk. My much beloved one. How are you. It was so nice to hear from you. We are all well and walk around the yard a lot, slide down the hill. These days it is very cold, so Mama is staying at home. You will probably get this card in February already, therefore I congratulate you with [your] day of the angel, may God help you in the future and bless you. We remember you a lot. The other day I wrote to Ak. Iv., don't know if he got it. I am happy for Seryozha. May the Lord help you in all your journeys, do not be lonesome my sweet, God will make it all well and we will be together again. I kiss you affectionately like I love you. Your M.

Letter from Anastasia to a friend at the infirmary. 20 February, 1918. Tobolsk.

[...] It is so sad to hear that Nikolai Nikolaevich Vasiliev died. We all find it hard [to think] that he is not alive. Friends write to us, but many letters don't reach us [...]. We remember the old days, visiting our infirmary. I guess no one goes to the graves of our wounded now – nearly everyone was taken away from Tsarskoe. Do you remember Lukyanov – he was pitiful and sweet, always playing with our bracelets like a baby. His visiting card is in my album, but unfortunately the album was left behind at Tsarskoe. Just now I am writing in our bedroom. On the writing desk are pictures of our beloved infirmary [...]. All in all, the times we visited the infirmary were awfully good. We often reminisce about our visits to the infirmary, the evening chats on the telephone, and everything, everything...

Letter from Maria to Ksenia Alexandrovna in Crimea. Tobolsk.

21 February, 1918. Thank you so much, Aunt Ksenia, darling for the card. I gave Papa the letter, now sending you the response. – Today the weather is wonderful, this morning I sat at the entrance and baked in the sun. It is even more boring in the garden now, they took down the hill, not completely but it is not good for sliding anymore. – They brought a lot of fire wood and Papa saws it, we help him. This year we learned to

chop and saw. And what do you do. How are you. Does Grandmama go out into fresh air. – We plan to sing during the service, started to practice, but the regent did not come yet, so we are not sure if we can sing on Saturday. Almost every Sunday we put on small plays. We have run out of all the reserves[201] so will have to start all over again. I don't know when you will get this letter, they say that mail is almost not working at all, but we continue to receive letters. The sisters are interfering with my writing, as they are shoving and talking loudly. In general when the four of us are sitting in our room, it becomes very noisy. We sing good songs, mimic the zurna and etc. and it comes out rather well. Papa and the sisters are going for a walk and are calling me. Do you recognize these physiognomies[202]. This was taken in the summer. Isa was not allowed here yet, and probably won't be. She gives English lessons here. All the best to you, my dear. I kiss you and everyone affectionately. May Christ be with you.   Your Maria.

"Do you recognize these physiognomies. This was taken in the summer." Anastasia, Tatiana, Olga, and Maria, whose heads were shaved due to measles.

---

[201] She means the scripts for plays.

[202] Maria attached to this letter a small photo of herself and her sisters with their heads shaved.

Letter from rom Maria to a friend. 22 February/7 March[203]. Tobolsk.

[...] In the evenings we get together to work or play cards - bridge or some other games, though I am particularly interested in [card games]. Papa reads [to us] out loud. Pretty often, when all 4 of us get together in a proper mood we sing various nice songs. This always results in us loudly imitating zurna sounds. Some of us knock against the door or any other object that catches our eye in order to produce more noise [...] and [we] create a hubbub that can be heard almost all over the house.

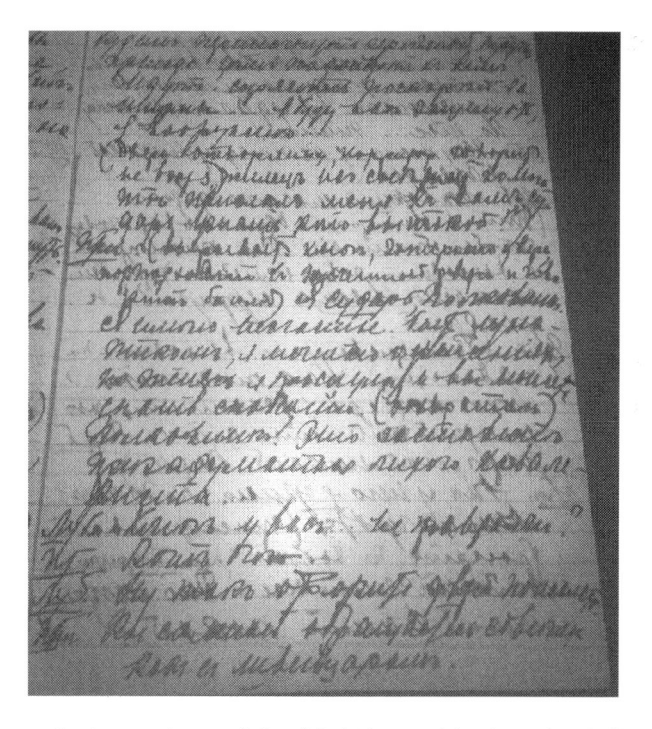

"Almost every Sunday we put on small plays." Script for one of the plays written in Olga's hand.

---

[203] The double dates are for old and new style calendars (Julian and Gregorian), the latter was instated in Russia at around this time.

From Anastasia to Ksenia Alexandrovna in Crimea.

Tobolsk 8/21 March 1918. My darling, sweet Aunt Ksenia. Thanks so much for the postcard which just arrived. For now we are alive and in good health, thank God. We are always so glad when we get news from you. How is Grandmama's health? We often reminisce and talk about you all. These days it's almost always sunny here and it's getting warm – quite pleasant! So we do our best to get out into the fresh air more. We can't slide down the mountain anymore (though it's still standing) as they've wrecked it and put a drainage ditch through it and so we cannot slide down on it. Well, they seem to have calmed down about it now because it was an eyesore for many for some time. It's truly foolish and pathetic. Well, we found new things to do. We saw, chop and split firewood and this is a useful and enjoyable task. We are already quite good at it. By doing this we help many and for us it is a pastime. We shovel the paths and the porch – we have become custodians! I have not yet turned into an elephant, though I might very soon. I really don't know all of a sudden – maybe it's too little exercise, though I don't know[204]. Please forgive my shocking handwriting – my hand moves something dreadful. We're all fasting this week and sing hymns by ourselves at home. Finally we were able to go to church! And we can have communion there. Well, how are you all and how are you all getting on? Nothing in particular has happened with us that I need to write about. I must finish now as we are going out to our yard to work, etc. We all hug you tightly, and I do too, and so do all the rest of us! Goodbye darling Aunty! May God save you! Everyone thanks you very much for your greetings and they send their regards to you too.   Your loving A.

---

[204] At this time, it seems that Maria gained a lot of weight.

"...We do our best to get out into the fresh air more". Olga, Nicholas, Anastasia and Tatiana in Tobolsk. Possibly Maria took this photo.

Letter from Anastasia to unknown friend. March 25. 1918 Tobolsk.

For the moment, thank God, we are living well. A detachment of the Red Army men came from Omsk, up until now they behaved themselves, and on the whole everything is calm. In the first week of Lent, we fasted and they let us go to church. At all the services through the week we sang by ourselves, as it is difficult to get the cloisters to come over with such frequency for services at home. Lessons for us are every day as usual, morning and evening. The weather has been wonderful these last few days and we often sit on the balcony, glad of change of scenery, looking at passers-by. Right now, I am sitting and writing by the window. It is already 7.45, but it is still light outside.

The church bells are tolling, which reminds us of the cathedral at Tsarskoe[205]. We've become regular custodians. We cleared the snow out of the yard where we go for walks, and now it is not so messy. Then we sometimes chop and saw wood – it is all going well with us.

Letter from Maria to V.G. Kapralova. 29 March/11 April, 1918.

29th March, 1918. I thank you so much, my good Vera Georgievna, for your letter No. 10. I did not respond to it on the same day as Anastasia, as in my opinion it is more fun for you not to get two [letters] at the same time, but one at a time. Vera Nikolaevna wrote to us, she said that she wrote us letters from your name but we never got them. Now she writes to us here, it is faster. – Where is Elena Nikolaevna now? Since we got here, we know nothing of her. Does she write to you at all? I remember last year and your sweet letters, and El.[ena] Nik.[olaevna]'s, [I] reread them when I have free time. Do any of [our] former wounded write to you? Anastasia got a very sweet card for her birthday, from Petrenko. He is at home. The weather is nice here, these days [we] had a bit of frost, but before that it was warming up already, and we baked in the sun a lot. [We] reminisced about the [snow] tower, the one near [our] dear cozy infirmary. When one starts to remember it all, and everything that happened there, one transports to T.S. and then it feels so strange that we are so far away in T.[obolsk]. What are you doing, my dear, and how do you live? If you visit the Sidorovs, give them regards from us and the same to other acquaintances. Do you know anything about where A.A. Miller is? I received your letters Nos. 1, 2, 3, 4, 8, 10, so unfortunately 4 [of the letters] got lost. And

---

[205] Feodorovsky Cathedral

you my dears? – In our mundane lives we are always happy to get letters. The sisters send regards. Anastasia and I embrace you affectionately. May God keep you. Maria.

Letter from Maria to V.G. Kapralova.

5/18 April, 1918. We send you, dear Vera Georgievna, a package with food. I hope that it will get there, but probably not until after a month. The other day we wrote to you, did you receive it? Your letters get here, but not all. Everything is fine here, thank God. All the best for now, we kiss you affectionately. Hearfelt regards to your sister from us. May God keep you. M.

Author's Note

The first Bolshevik party representatives arrived in Tobolsk in April of 1918.

Commissar Vasily Yakovlev inspected the house and met with the prisoners. He announced that he would be taking the former Emperor away from Tobolsk, but did not disclose the destination or the purpose. Assuming that he was being taken to Moscow to sign a separate peace with Germany, Nicholas tried to object, but it was futile. Since Aleksei was too ill to travel at the time, it was decided that Alexandra and Maria would accompany the Tsar, while Olga, Tatiana and Anastasia would stay in Tobolsk with their brother until he felt well enough to travel.

Letter from Anastasia to Nicholas II.[206] Tobolsk. 12th/25th April, 1918. My dear Papa! May the Lord and all the Saints protect you, my dear and beloved Papa. In our thoughts and prayers we are always with you. I cannot even imagine how we can be without you. I believe and hope that the Lord will help us all. Good night my precious and wonderful Papa. I send you 1000 big big kisses, as big as my love is for you. May the Lord be with you and bless you, darling[207]. Your loyal and faithful   Shvybz / Anastasia

Letter from Maria to Anastasia. 15/28 April, 1918.

Ekaterinburg, 28 April. Xpuctoc Bockpece![208] I send you my greetings for the Feast of Light, my sweet Anastasia. We arrived here by car after the train. We had breakfast at 4.30 in the cafeteria. Only unpacked our things in the evening, because the luggage was searched, even the "medicines" and the "candy"[209]. After two days in a cart with bumps our belongings were in terrible shape. Such an extraordinary thing though – the frames and perfume bottles were not broken, only the top of the Malzeket [210] spilled out, which stained the books, but Nyuta[211] and Sednev put everything back in order. Even inside the bags there was dust and dirt and all the wrapping paper was untidy and torn. We had tea together at 9.30 in the evening. After that we rested a little, we put up camp

---

[206] The Tsar would receive this letter some time after their arrival in Ekaterinburg.

[207] This sentence was written in English

[208] Christ Has Risen! (Russian)

[209] Code words for jewelry

[210] Possibly name of a perfume.

[211] Anna Demidova, the maid who accompanied them to Ekaterinburg, and later perished with the imperial family.

beds ourselves and went to bed at 11 o'clock. Papa read the gospel of the week to us. Mama teased Mashka, successfully imitating Pankra[tov]'s[212] enthusiasm, but despite all of that, everything again is a little depressing. We have not unpacked everything, because we were told that we would be moved to another place. I am not going to write to anyone else, so please give my Easter wishes to all and tell them that I send them my heartfelt regards. Tell Madelen and the others how we live. My best wishes to my dear Shvybz. May God protect you. Your M.

Postcard from Maria to Anastasia in Tobolsk.

Ekaterinburg, April 19th/May 2nd, 1918. [To] An.[astasia] N.[ikolaevna] Хрuстос Воскресе[213], my little and dear soul. I kiss you three times. I hope you receive all my little eggs and icons. We think about you all the time and dream about the happy day when we will see each other again. Did you receive all our letters? It is already a week and we have not seen each other and we have written [to you] every day. It is silly, what there is to write about, but we cannot write everything. There were some amusing incidents. Every night I wish you a good night's sleep. And you? In the entire house there is no water and we wait a long time for the samovar to be brought in, which is slow to heat. Mama has her meals in the camp bed and I have mine with Papa, Nyuta, Evg. Serg.[214], Sednev and Chemod[urov][215] in the dining room and Nyuta sleeps there. She

---

[212] Head of the guard there.

[213] Christ Has Risen (Russian).

[214] Dr Evgeni Sergeevich Botkin, who also accompanied the family into exile, and will later lose his his along with them.

[215] Servants who will aso perish with the family.

sends her greetings to all of you. Does little Tresses and the "good Russians" still take walks together?[216]

Author's Note

Those who remained in Tobolsk did not learn what was happening to their loved ones for almost two weeks after their departure. On May 7th they finally received the letters and learned that Nicholas, Alexandra and Maria had been taken to Ekaterinburg, a city in the Urals which was always hostile to the Tsar. They were imprisoned at the house that belonged to engineer Ipatiev, which was ominously referred to by the Bolsheviks as "The House of Special Purpose". Numerous letters between the family members started to fly back and forth during this time of separation.

Letter from Anastasia to Maria. 24 April/ 7 May. Tobolsk.

Indeed He Has Risen! My good Mashka Darling. We were so terribly happy to get the news [from you] and shared our impressions! I apologize for writing crookedly on the paper, but this is due to my foolishness. We received [a letter] from Al.Pav., very sweet, [he sends] regards to you, etc. How are you all? What about Sashka and T.P.? You see of course that there are always so many rumors; well you understand how hard it is and one doesn't know whom to believe and it is all so disgusting! As half of it is nonsense. But since there is nothing else, we believe it. Kl.[avdia] Mikh.[ailovna][217] comes to sit

---

[216] Possibly some sort of code language agreed upon by the family.

[217] Bitner.

with the little one. Aleksei is so sweet for a boy and tries so [hard]... (remember how it was on the little bench when you were here?). We take turns having breakfast with Aleks.[ei] and making him eat, although there are days when he eats without encouragement. We are always with you in our thoughts, dear ones. It is terribly sad and empty; I really don't know what is going on. The baptismal cross is with us, of course, and we got your news, so the Lord will help and is helping. We arranged the iconostasis awfully nicely for Easter, all in spruce, the way it should be here, and the flowers. We took pictures. I hope they come out. I continue to draw, not too badly they say, so it's very pleasant. We swung on the swings, and when I fell it was such a wonderful fall!... Yes, indeedy! I told the sisters about this so many times yesterday, that they got tired of hearing about it, but I could tell it again and again, although there is no one left to tell. In general, there is a whole trainload of things to tell you all. My "Jimmy" woke up and is coughing, so he is sitting at home and we both send regards. Such weather it was! One could just shout from the pleasantness of it. Strangely enough, I tanned more deeply than anyone else, a regular acrobat[218] woman!? But these days are boring and not nice, it is cold, and this morning we froze, but of course still did not go back inside... I very much apologize [that I] forgot to send good wishes to all you dear ones for the holiday; I kiss you all not thrice but lots of times. We all thank you my darling, for the letters. There were manifestations here too - but rather weak[219]. We sit here together as always, but you are missed in the room. Tell the precious Papa that we are very grateful for the smock; we use it tastefully - I apologize of course that

---

[218] She may mean "Arab woman".

[219] She is probably referring to May Day demonstrations.

this is such a jumbled letter you understand that my thoughts are racing and I cannot write everything so I jump on whatever comes to mind. Soon we will go for a walk, summer has not arrived yet and nothing is blooming, it is being a real slouch. I want to see you all so much, (you know) it's sad! I am going for a walk, well I am back. It's boring whether one goes out or not. We swung. The sun came out but it's cold and my hand can barely write, Alexander Al. – there there do you understand Hello.[220]   My sweet dear ones, how we pity you all. We trust that the Lord will help - His very own - !!!... I am unable and cannot say what I want, but you will understand I hope. Your regards were transmitted [to us] word for word, and we send you big thanks and the same. It is so pleasant here, they bless one in almost all the churches, it ends up being very cozy. Sasha and her girlfriends told us that they were cold and hungry and [that] they almost got killed, poor things, they are a little curious as to what they are guilty of and for what, it's unclear. Yesterday we went to see the baby piglets. There is mud in our little garden, but it froze up now. So boring, no news from Katya for a terribly long time. Such a laugh from the journey… I would need to tell you this in person, and laugh. We just had tea. Alek.[sei] is with us and we just devoured so many Paskas[221] that I plan to burst. When we sing amongst ourselves, it comes out badly because we need a fourth voice, but you are not here and therefore we make terribly witty comments about this. Much weaker but we have funny anecdotes too. In the evenings we sit around at […], yesterday we read fortunes using the book. You know the one, and sometimes we work [...]. We did all you asked [.. .] Kisses to you, and all you dear ones, and much

---

[220] This expression was often repeated in their letters, most likely some sort of agreed upon code language.

[221] Special Easter cake.

else and etc., I will not elaborate, for you will understand. Thoughts of long ago... Russa, although she is sweet, but [she] is strange and makes one angry, for she doesn't understand and one simply cannot bear it. Once I was almost rude [to this] cretin. Well, it looks like I have written enough foolishness. Right now I will write some more, and then I will read a bit, [it is] so nice to have free time. Goodbye for now. I wish you all the best, happiness, and all good things. We constantly pray for you and think [of you], may the Lord help. May Christ be with you, precious ones. I embrace you all very tightly... and kiss you...   [Anastasia]

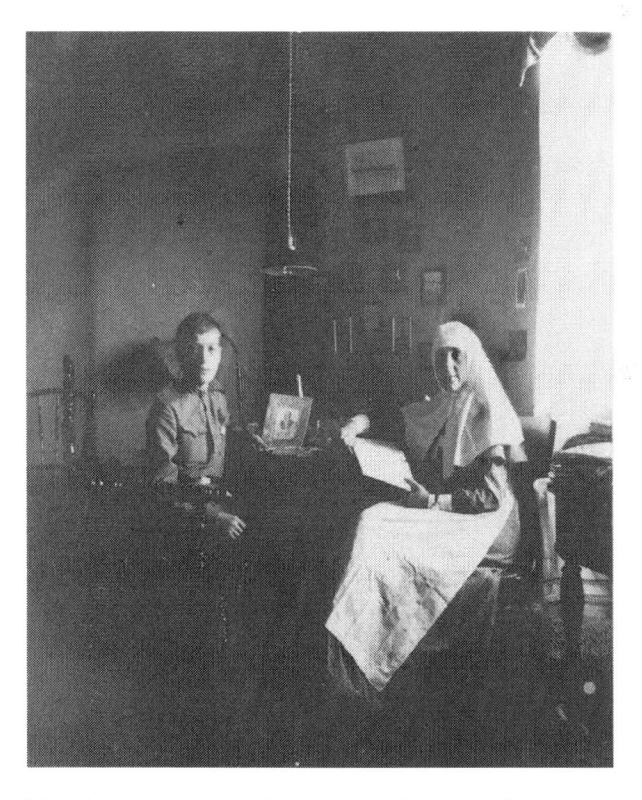

"Kl.[avdia] Mikh.[ailovna] comes to sit with the little one. Aleksei is so sweet for a boy and tries so [hard]" "
K.M. Bitner with Aleksei.

Letter from Anastasia to Alexandra. 25 April/8 May, 1918. Tobolsk.

Beloved and dear Mama. Enormous thanks for the letters. You have no idea how much happiness this letter brought us. I hope that your heart is not too bad and you have no more headaches. What happened with Garad is very sad and hurtful but it seems to me that he was quite an idiot. We had tea today as usual with Zhylik, who tormented and crushed us terribly. We spend the evenings working with Nast.[asia][222], who kisses your hands, and sometimes play bezique. We have the evening tea early and in the dining room. It is very nice to have a church here. It is very sad without you, my dear ones. All the time we feel that something is missing. The boats have now started to sail and we often hear their sirens. This noise is so familiar, do you remember? There are a lot of things that we would love to know about you, our infinitely dear ones. How do you feel and what is going on now? We need to go downstairs for dinner and Olga will stay with the little one. Bronislav and his wife send regards to you. He has recovered, thank God, and goes for walks. Kay wrote, she sent us her good wishes and kisses. Her grandmother is dying, her mother has gone to be with her but now she returned. Goodbye for now, my immensely dear Mama. You are constantly in our thoughts, our precious ones and we pray for you. May the Lord and Saint Ioann of Tobolsk protect all of you.   Good night, I kiss you three very affectionately my dear ones, how I love you ++++. May the Lord come to your aid.   Your faithful A. My good thoughts to everyone.

Letters from Maria to Tobolsk.

---

[222] Anastasia Hendrikova.

Ekaterinburg, 26th April/9th May, 1918. Thank you, our little souls, for the telegram which we received yesterday before dinner; we are very happy because this is the first news we received from you since we [got] here. We are happy to learn that you received our letters. Do you remember, Shvybz, our special corner near Feodorovsky Sobor, of T.G. [?] and of his students "Bokche" and of others; the story of the parrot that Al.[eksei] told us and [which] always pleased Nyuta? We began to look like Vl.Al., do you understand?[223] Do not forget one of you to ask for the address of P.Iv. and Styopa. Our life continues without changes. Yesterday we walked for such a long time in the little garden, because the weather was better and the sun warmed us – this reminded us of last summer at Tsarkoe Selo. We thought a lot about you, when we were listening to a polka at the station waiting room. Afterwards, someone sang a duet. Does Maksimochin still sing so loudly that the entire Tobolsk can hear? It is a shame that we do not know the words to "I do not mind". You could probably ask for the words and of other songs. Time goes by so fast that I haven't had time to read, not even once, the words of the songs that we wrote down. Write to M. Zizi and Maria Nik. and tell them that we kiss [them] and think about them. I hope that Ch. wrote to all the sisters. Have you had news from Zinochka? While I write, Papa organizes his cigarettes that were packed loosely together during the journey but were not totally damaged. Papa kisses you all. A big "good morning" to A.A.[224]. You will see him tomorrow for sure. We have retained good memories of him. What do Baby[225] and the others do? [...] We think about everybody with affection. We talk a lot about you and think about you all the time,

---

[223] Probably more code language.

[224] Alexei Volkov

[225] Aleksei

dear ones. We wait for a letter from you. I kiss you affectionately, my precious ones. May the Lord protect you+++ Your Masha. It seems to me that you are being formal in using "Vous" in your letter. What became of Jimmy, Joy and Ortipo[226]?

Ekaterinburg. 27 April/ 10 May, 1918. We miss the quiet and peaceful life in Tobolsk. Here we have unpleasant surprises almost daily. Just now the members of regional committee were here and asked each of us how much money we had with us. We had to sign off on it. As you know, Papa and Mama did not even have one kopek with them so they signed, nothing, and I [had] 16 r.[ubles] 75 k.[opeks], which Anastasia gave me for the road. They took all the money from the rest to [give to the] committee for safekeeping, left each one a little, - gave them receipts. They warn [us] that we are not guaranteed not to have new searches. – Who would have thought that after 14 months of captivity they treat us this way. - We hope that things are better for you, the way it was when we were there. Yesterday, we did not have time to send the letter because the guards were changed three times. I hope that today the letter can be sent. All new guards came inside and checked everything. Each time, Mama was obliged to get up from [her] bed and greet the guards in her dressing gown. Yesterday an extraordinary event happened: Nyuta and I washed Mama's hair. Everything went well and her hair was not tangled, but I don't know what is going to happen today and everything for sure is going to come undone. The water here is very good, almost as good as in Tsarskoe Selo. In the bathtub the water looks light blue. Yesterday we went for a walk, like every day, until tea time. The sun was very warm, just like in Tobolsk, and in the evening it penetrated the windows of the second floor. We hope Kolya comes to play with you. I

---

[226] The family's dogs they brought into exile with them. Only Joy survived the execution.

am ending the letter because there is nothing else to say. I hold you in my arms, my little souls. Warm wishes to everybody. May Christ be with you +   Masha

28 Apr. [11 May, 1918]. Good morning my dears. Just got up and started the fire in the stove, as it got cold in the rooms. The wood is crackling cozily, it reminds [me] of a frosty day in T[obolsk]. – Today we gave our dirty laundry to the washerwoman. Nyuta has become a washerwoman too, washed Mama's kerchief, and very well too, and the dust rags. – For a few days now we have Letts as guards here. It is probably not very cozy by you, everything is packed. Did you pack my things, if you have not packed the book for birth then ask N.T. to write. If it does not work out, it's fine. You will probably arrive soon now. – We do not know anything about you, waiting for a letter very impatiently.   I continue to draw everything from Bem's book. Maybe you can buy some white paint for me. We have very little of it here. In the autumn Zhylik got hold of some good one, flat and round. – Who knows, maybe this letter will reach you just as you are departing. May the Lord bless your journey and keep you from all evil. I want to know very much who will escort you. Affectionate thoughts and prayers surround you – just so we may be together once again. I kiss you affectionately, my sweet dears, and bless you +. Heartfelt regards to all and to those who are remaining too.   I hope that Al.[eksei] is feeling stronger and the trip will not tire him out too much. This morning we will take a walk as it is warm. – Valya[227] is still not allowed here. – Tell Al. [?] regards to you and others. Such a pity that I was not able to say goodbye. It will probably be so awfully sad for you to leave that cozy house, etc., I keep remembering all the cozy rooms and the garden. Do you still swing or did the board break? – Papa and I kiss you

---

[227] Prince Valya Dolgorukov

warmly. – May God keep you +. I send regards to all in the house. Does Tolya still come over to play? All the best and [I] wish you a good journey if you are departing. Your M.

Letter from Maria to Tatiana in Tobolsk.

Ekaterinburg, 2nd May/15th May, 1918. Papa thanks you for your letter, Tatiana, my little soul. We have read it time and again with great pleasure. We strongly doubt that they will send us to another place. If only!!! they would let you all to come to us. However it would be necessary to accommodate all female staff, ten persons, in the big living room, where at this moment Sednev and Chemod.[urov] are. You three [would live] beside the bedroom, where the washroom is. Between these rooms, the doors were removed, big doors! If we open the blocked room, we could accommodate Aleksei and Nagorny there. On our floor there are only two other rooms, if they give them to us, in the one where the furnace is, we could put Vl.Nik.[228], Zhylik and Mr. Gibbes, and in the other – where there is a little trapdoor, we could accommodate Tatishev[229]. We were told nothing about Valya[230]. The house was built on a slope, but there are two floors on the side of the garden. Downstairs is the kitchen and the guards' rooms; we do not know how many rooms are downstairs, or how the male personnel will be lodged. Downstairs there is a banya, which does not function. Upstairs where we are, there is [one] good bathroom for the entire house. Here there are no camp beds, no pillows, no wash bowls, no bed linen or table linen. In fact, there is nothing, so you need to bring

---

[228] Dr Vladimir Nikolaevich Derevenko

[229] Count Dmitri Tatishev- Lieutenant in the Preobrazhensky Guard.

[230] Count Valentin Dolgorukov.

everything. Where we will put your luggage, I have no idea. Ours is, at the moment in the living room. There is a lot of dust, we acquired a broom and Nyuta sweeps all day long. Aunt Ella lives in Perm for sure, because yesterday we read in the papers that she was sent out of the capital. All my best wishes, my dear Tatiana.

Letter from Maria to Aleksei in Tobolsk.

Ekaterinburg, 2nd May/15th May, 1918. Papa and Mama thank you very much for your letters, my precious Aleksei. It is with joy that we read and reread your dear lines. We were happy to hear that you help with all the chores and that you go out in the yard. We hope that you sit in the sun now. Yesterday, they bought us a good samovar, bigger than Nyuta's one, it is pleasant to have one of our own. Before we had to share one with the guard squad and we had to wait for it for a long time. They bring us breakfast from the cafeteria but for Mama, Sednev prepares macaroni, vermicelli, rice, as well as eggs, on the alcohol stove. Did you color the eggs for Easter? Oh, how we would love to be with you, and not here! These days the sun warms us very well. I am writing to you in the morning, Papa is just going to start reading, [while] sitting at the table. Mama is still in bed. Today I am alone and will write to you all. It is difficult to write anything pleasant, because there is very little of it here to report, but on the other hand, God does not abandon us, the sun shines and the birds sing. This morning we heard church bells. That was the only pleasant and agreeable event. We were happy to learn that Al.P.[231] sold the pigs so successfully. What is he going to do with the piglets? Mama, speaking of the turkey, said "you should not have...". At this time she is getting

---

[231] Kirpichnikov

out of bed and I will do her hair. We had washed her hair remarkably well with the "Cow"[232]. My dear, how I would love to see you. I hope you feel better quickly and start running around again. I hold you very tightly in my arms, my dear little brother. How is Zhylik's cough? May Christ protect you.   Your Masha+

Letter from Maria to Tobolsk.

Ekaterinburg, 3rd May/16th May, 1918. I write to you in semi-darkness as we do not have any light because the windows have been whitewashed. The white color is very unpleasant. It is, above all, bad for Mama because she suffers constantly from headaches. Sednev has been in bed with the flu for the last two days. This evening he had temperature of 38.6. He is so tall that he has to bend his legs on the camp bed and is obliged to lie down curled up.   Nyuta asks you to bring an electric iron in your hand luggage. Yesterday, we were only allowed to go for a walk in the afternoon. When the walk ended we came in and hot cocoa was waiting for us.   Many words of goodbye for Shvybz have been put together[233]. Tell this to Kay, because I have not written to her and send her best wishes from us here. Have you already received our letter, written during our journey where we speak about Nik.[olai] Yak.[ovlevich]. We have not understood the one where Dusya got married and how it is unexpected for Lyuba. Thank you for the Nik. Dem.[234] news. I had a dream about Mitya, who was just going to whitewash glass doors, in a long corridor with a big brush. This is it... I was very upset because of the whitewashed windows, yesterday. Mama, saw Gabk's secretary in a

---

[232] Nyuta?

[233] Code language

[234] Demenkov

dream, who was sending his best wishes. Shvybz's letter, which delighted Nyuta, [it] was read several times. She greets you and the others. We cannot understand the absence of little Tresses[235]. Is Godmother still living in Petersburg? I am going to take a deep breath – maybe we will receive letters from you, because yesterday we did not receive any. Of course we do not doubt that you have written to us every day. In the mornings, Papa reads to us, The Acts of the Apostles and The Gospels. I am continuing this letter after lunch, at 2.30. Nyuta and I played solitaire in the sitting room. We are getting ready to go for a walk at three o'clock. Outside today it seems to be colder, but we do not know exactly because the thermometer is indecipherable. Last year on this day it rained heavily, and we still went for a walk. Ask Shvybz and the others if they remember. Here, we just returned from our walk. The weather became mild but gloomy. I believe that today we will wait for your letter in vain - I have concluded!!! Ask Tatiana to look for the large ivory rosary, to have it blessed and sent to Aunt Ella in Perm[236]. We kiss you affectionately and bless you all, our dear ones. May God protect you. Your M. We received from Aunt Ella: three eggs, coffee and chocolate. Did Kolk's daughter receive our wishes for the holidays? To all lots of good wishes, etc.

Letter from Maria to Elizabeth Feodorovna. 4/17 May, 1918.

He Has Risen Indeed! We kiss you thrice, dearest. Thank you very much for the eggs, chocolate, coffee. Mama drank her first cup of coffee with great pleasure, it was very good. It's very good for her headaches, and as it happens we had not taken any with us.

---

[235] Possibly code language

[236] She was actually moved to Alapaevsk, not far from Ekaterinburg.

We learned from the newspapers that you had been sent away from your convent, and were very sad for you. It is strange that we should all end up in the same province under arrest[237]. We hope that you will be able to spend the summer somewhere out of town, in Verkhoturie or in some monastery. We have so missed having a church. My address is: Ekaterinburg, the Regional Executive Committee, to the Chairman, for transmission to me. May God keep you +   Your loving goddaughter

Letter from Maria to Z. S. Tolstaya.

Ekaterinburg, 4/17 May, 1918. Christ Has Risen!   My dear Z. Good wishes to you for the bright holiday. I apologize for [writing] so late, but we departed right before the holidays. It was very unexpected for us. Aleksei happened to be sick, so the sisters had to stay with him. They are supposed to arrive here soon. Tell Rita that not that long ago we saw the little Sedusha. Today is three weeks since we left Tobolsk. It is so sad to be without the others, especially now during the holidays. We have settled in nicely here. The house is small but clean, shame that it's right in the city so the garden is rather small. When the others arrive, not sure how we will settle, there are not that many rooms. I live with Papa and Mama in one, where we spent almost the entire day. Just now we went out into the garden, the weather is gray and it is raining. On the way, the weather was wonderful. We rode horses for 260 versts[238] until Tyumen. The roads were awful, we were jolted terribly. The paper with which our things were wrapped rubbed out in places. Tobacco fell out of the cigarettes. But strangely no glass broke. We took the

---

[237] Grand Duchess Elizabeth was also murdered by the Bolsheviks that summer, along with other Romanov grand dukes.

[238] One verst is equal to 1.0668 km/ 0.6629 mile/ 3,500 feet.

medicines with us and arrived safely. Rode for two days, stayed the nights in a village. Took horses across the Irtysh, and walked across the Tura[239] on foot and a few sazhens[240] to the banks – in a ferry. Mama withstood the journey surprisingly well, but now of course feels tired and has a headache almost daily. Doctor Botkin came with us, the poor man had kidney colics on the way, he was suffering a lot. We stopped in a village and they put him to bed there, he rested for two hours and continued with us. Luckily the pains did not happen again. And how are you all? The sisters wrote to you, that we got news from you. If you want to write to me, my address is: Ekaterinburg, the Regional Executive Committee. To the Chairman, to be given to me. Have you had any news from Tili. Regards to all yours and Nik. Dm. I kiss you, Rita and the children affectionately. I wish you all the best. May the Lord keep you. It was terribly sad that we were not able to go to the cathedral even once and venerate the relics of St. Ioann of Tobolsk.

Author's Note

About a month after Maria, Alexandra and Nicholas were taken to Ekaterinburg, Aleksei finally felt well enough to travel and he and his three sisters were escorted to Ekaterinburg. Regrettably, there is not enough concrete information about the family's Ekaterinburg imprisonment, as there were almost no letters going out from the Ipatiev house after the rest of the children arrived there. This period is basically known only by the brief entries in the diaries of Nicholas and Alexandra, as well as a few testimonies of

---

[239] Irtysh and Tura are rivers.

[240] A sazhen is equal roughly to 7 feet.

some witnesses. We do know however, that conditions in the "House of Special Purpose", as it was known, were much worse than anything the family had experienced in Tobolsk . There were 12 guards who lived in the same house and ate at the same table with the family. Commissar Avdeyev, who was in charge liked to degrade the prisoners daily. Reportedly they all put up with hardship and endured humiliation with gentle submission, and in their almost total isolation from everyone and everything they showed grace and fortitude. The prisoners were still allowed to walk in the small garden, but only once a day: at first for about fifteen minutes, later for no more than five. Only a few retainers were allowed to stay with the family once they were all moved to Ekaterinburg: Dr Evgeny Botkin, Anna Demidova, Ivan Kharitonov, Alexei Trupp and the kitchen boy Lyonka Sednev. Dr. Botkin served as a sort of an intermediary between the family members and the commissar, and tried to defend them from abuse the best he could. Botkin and the three servants were all murdered along with the family they served so faithfully. The boy Sednev was spared because he was only 13 years old – the same age as Aleksei.

It is impossible to say whether in the last months of their lives any of the prisoners thought about the possibility of execution, but there is some evidence that even the 13 year old Aleksei at least considered it. Reportedly he once said: "If they kill us, I hope that we are not tortured..." After some time, as they got to know the family, their rough guards gradually softened towards the prisoners - they were quite surprised by the simplicity and dignity of the former imperial family. Towards the end, even Avdeyev was replaced by Yakov Yurovsky, presumably because he was thought to have become too sympathetic towards his imperial captives and was no longer trusted to carry out their execution properly.

Anastasia aboard "The Rus"- the ship that brought her and her three siblings to Ekaterinburg to rejoin their parents and Maria. This is believed to be one of the last photos of Anastasia.

From Alexandra's diary. 5/18 June, 1918. Anastasia's last birthday.

Anastasia's 17th birthday. +17 °. Beautiful weather. Children continued to roll out the dough and prepare bread, it is now baking. Baby was brought to us early. T. read to me some Spiritual readings, while I worked. +28 °. 1 o'cl. Lunch - excellent bread. 3 1/4 [o'clock]. Rolled Baby out to the garden, and we all sat there for an hour - very hot, beautiful lilac bushes and small - honeysuckle foliage is beautiful, but, as usual, not well-groomed. Rested, I'm tired, it's hard to breathe. 8 o'cl. Dinner. Played cards with Baby, then he was taken to his room. Played bezique with N. A brief storm, but the rooms are very stuffy. The good nuns now send milk and eggs for us and Aleksei, and cream.

This is also believed to be one of the last photos of Anastasia before her death.

From Nicholas's diary. 14/27 June, 1918. Maria's last birthday.

Our dear Maria has reached her 19th year. The weather stayed the usual tropical, 26° in the shade, and inside 24°, even hard to tolerate! Spent an anxious night and stayed awake and dressed… All this was because the other day we received two letters, one after the other, which informed us to get ready to be kidnapped by some loyal people! But the days passed and nothing happened, and the anticipation and uncertainty were extremely torturous.

Author's Note

Preparations for the family's execution began in July, in secret from the prisoners. In the middle of the night from 16th to 17th July, Commandant Yakov Yurovsky awakened the family and told them that they had to be moved to a "safer place". After everyone got dressed, they were ushered into the semi-cellar of the Ipatiev house, walking down the stairs and outside through a small courtyard. Everyone remained outwardly calm. Nicholas was carrying Aleksei, who although by now was taller than his father, was once again too ill to walk by himself. The rest of the family and the servants were carrying small items like pillows. Anastasia clutched her little pet dog, Jimmy. Once in the cellar room, Aleksei and Alexandra were given chairs to sit on, as neither was able to stand for a long period of time. The rest stood around them in a row. It is believed that the prisoners were told that a photo of them was requested by the Moscow Soviet to dispel rumors that they had escaped. This was probably done to ensure that everyone was arranged in a way most conducive to efficient shooting. After a few minutes, the entire family, along with the doctor and servants, were brutally shot and bayoneted to death.

Semi-cellar room at the Ipatiev House after the execution of Maria, Anastasia and their family.

List of books that belonged to Maria, found at the Ipatiev house

- "*On Paris*" by Avenarius. On the reverse side of the cover is written: "M. H. Christmas 1913 from N. V. P. "

- "*Visual Teaching of Foreign Languages*" On the reverse side of cover wrapper is the inscription: "Marie".

- "*Reflections*" by Popov – text book. The wrapping sheet it reads: "M. N. 1910."

- English book "*The Role and the Ring*", green cover with a picture.

Books that belonged to Anastasia, found at the Ipatiev house

- Four books of essays by Lazhechnikoa, Volumes 1-12, in colorful bindings.

Bibliography.

"Avgusteishiye Sestry Miloserdia" (The August Sisters of Mercy") by N. Zvereva

"Divny Svet" ("The Wonderous World") by Sr. Nektaria

Pered Rassrelom ("Before the Execution") by I. Nepein

"Russkaya Golgofa" (The Russian Golgotha") by V. Kuznetzov

Images are courtesy of GARF (The State Archive of Russian Federation) and Beinecke Library at Yale University.

Printed in Great Britain
by Amazon